Dramatizing Aesop's Fables

Creative Scripts
for the
Elementary Classroom

Louise Thistle

Dale Seymour Publications

To Charles, who keeps the child in me

alive and happy

About the Author: Louise Thistle is a freelance drama consultant who teaches elementary school students and preschool children how to dramatize stories and poems from literature. She also gives staff development training in dramatizing literature to teachers.

Louise received her B.A. in English and elementary education from Tufts University and her M.A. in drama with an emphasis in child drama from San Diego State University. She has taught elementary school in Massachusetts and California, has been an instructor of creative drama at San Diego State University, and an instructor of literature in the San Diego Community Colleges.

Louise also acts, directs, and writes plays. Her play, "Little Red Snares the Wolf," won first prize in London's Players/Playwrights Competition. It has been performed by schools in England and the U.S.

Managing Editor: Diane Silver
Product Manager: Bev Dana
Senior Editor: Lois Fowkes
Production/Manufacturing Manager: Janet Yearian
Production/Manufacturing Coordinator: Barbara Atmore
Design Manager: Jeff Kelly
Cover Design: Rachel Gage
Illustrations: Rachel Gage
Text Design: Jeff Kelly

Order number DS31209
ISBN 0-86651-653-0

2 3 4 5 6 7 8 9 10-BA-96 95 94 93

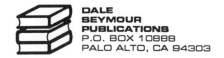

DALE
SEYMOUR
PUBLICATIONS
P.O. BOX 10888
PALO ALTO, CA 94303

Contents

Acknowledgments

I want to thank the many people who made this book possible. First my gratitude goes to Charles, to whom this book is dedicated. I am deeply indebted to artist and former teacher Emily Packer, who spent hundreds of hours making the many imaginative costume pieces and props that have so enchanted the children and the teachers who acted with them.

I am very grateful for the expert guidance and help of child drama director and university instructor Sharon Oppenheimer, who gave me many excellent suggestions that have enriched this book. I must thank Maria and Athan Anagnostopoulos, directors of The Greek Institute in Cambridge, Massachusetts, who gave me in-depth insight and background on Greek culture and art. They gave me the idea of using Aesop's fables as the unifying device for this book.

I thank Mary Troy, reading specialist with the South Bay Union School District, who read my first manuscript and offered much sound practical advice that I have incorporated here. I very much appreciate the support of Rosa Perez, director of PROJECT EXCEL, a Title VII federal grant to develop gifted potential in Hispanic students in San Diego City Schools. She gave me the opportunity to work with many excellent teachers of Limited English Proficient (LEP) students and the enthusiastic children in her project.

Thanks also to Karen Moffitt, San Diego City Schools teacher, who was so helpful and encouraging when I first began teaching literature dramatization to the gifted. Thank you to Professors Beverly Beem, Susan Gardner, and Nancy Cross, coordinators of the teachers' Writing, Reading, and Literature Workshop at Walla Walla College, who told me a book on this subject was very much needed.

Many thanks to Don Armin for his expert advice on how to make this book helpful to teachers, and to Jeanne Armin, my mentor in child drama, who inspired me to follow this profession. I also thank Dr. Maggi McKerrow, Professor of Drama at San Diego State University, for her guidance on my thesis, the seed for this book. I owe a debt of gratitude to music teacher Demi McNeil Wallace, who gave me many imaginative suggestions on incorporating and creating sound effects.

Others who helped me are Jean Stewart, director of the children's room of the San Diego Public Library, and staff members Linda Begley and Kathy Askin, who patiently fulfilled my many requests for books. I am grateful to Frieda Pallas, children's librarian at Point Loma Branch Library in San Diego, for her valuable suggestion to use acting captions with the illustrations. I owe a particularly deep debt of appreciation to Point Loma librarian Pat Katka, who has been continually interested and supportive of this project and who has always cheerfully and efficiently helped me obtain hard-to-find books.

I appreciate the contribution of Naomi Adler, storyteller/puppeteer/teacher at Polka Children's Theatre in London, England, for the design of the lion paper plate mask. Thank you to Jenny and Dudley Hartman for being so gracious with their time and computer expertise. Jack Sanford has shepherded this work. I appreciate very much the expert editorial assistance of Dale Seymour senior editor Lois Fowkes.

My mom and dad nurtured and encouraged my love of drama and the world of art and imagination. Most importantly, they showed me through their example the value of persistence.

I owe deep gratitude to the many teachers, librarians, professors of education, recreation directors, parents, and children who welcomed me into their class-rooms and centers and wholeheartedly participated in the drama. You are the ones for whom this book is written. Without you, it would not exist at all.

Louise Thistle

Introduction

This book came about as a result of teaching students from preschool to grade six how to dramatize literature. These students were mainstream, gifted, and limited and nonnative English speakers, as well as educationally and emotionally handicapped students. I saw how involved students became when acting out a story. The literature became personally meaningful to them; it became their own.

While teaching in schools, libraries, and community and recreation centers, I found that literature dramatization had many academic, psychological, and social benefits for both students and teachers. Drama integrates the language arts of speaking, listening, reading, writing, and literary analysis. Students must speak and listen to play their parts. They need and want to read the stories they will dramatize or have just dramatized. They must analyze and understand the characters and their situations to play their parts. Writing or discussing reactions to the drama and the characters is a natural follow-up. Comprehension is continually tested, because students must understand the literature in order to dramatize it.

Music, art, history, and science activities may be included in studying this material. For example, makeshift rhythm instruments can create sound effects. Students' art can illustrate the literature they so vividly experience. Students like to learn the history and background of an author or culture they will play. They also must examine an animal's behavior and bodily structure to play it. And of course, students are directly experiencing the art of the theatre by acting and sometimes directing.

Of all academic subjects, drama seems the most like real life. Consequently, drama is psychologically and socially meaningful to students — and very enjoyable. Limited and nonnative English speakers see and experience the characters and use the language in an exciting, purposeful way.

It is exhilarating and therapeutic to act powerful feelings and emotions in the classroom, a place where strong emotion is not often encouraged. Students can find comfort and liberation in realizing that we all share strong feelings of joy, sorrow, and struggle. Drama unites students and teachers, making everyone feel a sense of belonging to the human family.

Drama is a team art that bonds the group, giving students of different abilities and interests a natural way to work together. Often students who never noticed each other previously develop a new rapport as they act out a scene together.

Drama is energizing and develops student confidence. Despite a common misconception, a creative dramatic experience has a calming effect on students, making them more receptive to quiet, focused lessons.

Perhaps most importantly, literature dramatization is memorable and fun. Students never forget a piece of literature that they have dramatized, and they often ask to do it again and again.

Teachers in classrooms and those participating in workshops cite a variety of benefits of literature dramatization. They mention that it increases comprehension by giving students the experience of living through a piece of literature. Dramatizing literature reminds teachers that we learn best by doing and by being physically involved. Students who are rarely involved in other activities participate eagerly in dramatizing stories. Both shy and aggressive students, often outsiders, bloom and find a creative vent for their strong feelings. Those gifted in the affective domain, who are often disregarded in the academic setting, have a chance to shine. Teachers, too, like an activity in which everyone can participate and succeed on his or her own level.

The teachers who participated in the testing of this program wanted to do more literature dramatization in their classrooms. They needed simple methods and hands-on material to use in their classrooms immediately. They also requested material students could use to act out stories on their own in groups. Teachers wanted critical-thinking questions for writing and discussion. They wanted art, drama, and other follow-ups with each lesson to deepen students' understanding and appreciation of the literature. The result is this book, *Dramatizing Aesop's Fables*.

The stories in this book were adapted for use with the narrative-mime approach to dramatize a story. Narrative mime differs from the traditional play or readers' theatre script in that only the narrator reads from a script. The players hold no paper and are thus free to act using their whole bodies. To use the narrative-mime approach, a narrator (the teacher or a student) reads or tells the story while the students pantomime the actions, express the feelings, and repeat or ad-lib the dialogue. They also create sound effects to accompany the action.

Aesop's fables were chosen for adaptation because they are classics that have lasted 2500 years. Their characters, plots, and morals have been used by Aristotle, Shakespeare, La Fontaine, Benjamin Franklin, Walt Disney, and many others. The fables are short, funny, full of action, and have broad characters, making them ideal to begin a program of literature dramatization.

The fables appeal across the age range. Kindergartners and preschool children enjoy them for their funny animal characters, middle graders enjoy their bold, humorous actions, and older students and adults like their earthy, real characters and clever truths. With morals that are open to a variety of interpretations, the fables are a good vehicle for promoting critical thinking.

Using "Dramatizing Aesop's Fables" in the Classroom

Chapter 1 explains three principles students should follow for good acting. Following these principles will make the experience worthwhile and successful.

Chapter 2 discusses the mechanics of good acting, with tips and techniques on how to set up the classroom and conduct lessons so that the drama runs smoothly. The tips will help teachers elicit the best possible acting from their students. Teachers will also learn how to incorporate instruments, other sound effects, and simple costume pieces in a drama.

Chapter 3 describes how to dramatize stories using the narrative-mime approach with students ranging from preschoolers to students in upper grades. It includes ways to work in cooperative groups for different age levels.

Chapter 4 is a model introductory lesson in literature dramatization. It uses the fable "The Lion and the Mouse" in a first lesson that can be performed by all age levels and by Limited English Proficiency (LEP) students.

Chapter 5 is the heart of the book. Along with background material and critical-thinking questions about Aesop, it includes eight of Aesop's best-loved fables adapted for acting. These adapted fables include actions to do or feeling to express in almost every sentence. To motivate creative dramatics, each fable is illustrated with pictures of the characters in action. These pictures will help students to become the characters and to experience their dramatic moments. The pictures may also inspire students' own art. Each picture has questions on the page that ask students to show or tell the characters' actions or feelings.

Accompanying each fable are sections entitled Becoming the Character, which has activities to do in preparation for acting the story, and Re-enacting Moments from the Story, which has activities to deepen characterization and understanding. These activities, which are written directly to the student, can be used as an alternative to acting the whole story.

All stories have critical-thinking questions for writing or oral discussion, suggestions for research and reading, and art and drama follow-ups. Costume and sound-effects suggestions are included for each story.

Chapter 6 includes 27 more of Aesop's fables. This chapter explains how to adapt and act out these fables using the narrative-mime approach.

Chapter 7 describes ways to use the fables to develop reading skills. Students can turn the original fables into play scripts. Students can also use a shared-reading approach, with one student reading and the other student acting.

Chapter 8 contains critical-thinking questions, art, and writing and research projects that can be used with individual fables or used to compare and contrast many fables.

An annotated bibliography lists large collections of Aesop's fables (some researchers have attributed over 150 fables to Aesop) and picture books with one or several fables. The bibliography also includes books on creative drama with practical activities for the classroom teacher, and art books that show students how to draw cartoon and realistic animals.

I have had great pleasure seeing teachers and students of all abilities and backgrounds dramatize these stories. Their involvement has revitalized the fables for me and has demonstrated their enduring appeal. Aesop might have laughed with pleasure, because, as is true of all great humorists, he was a child at heart. May your students' dramatizations bring delight and joy to your classroom, too.

CHAPTER ONE

The Three Principles of Good Acting

Three simple principles are the foundation of a good acting program:
> **Believe** you are the part you are playing.
> Exercise **control** over your actions and emotions.
> Use **voice** and **movement** expressively to portray different characters and their feelings.

These principles are followed by all good actors. If students practice them, their acting will be successful and will improve. The experience will be satisfying for all concerned, and students will be participating wholeheartedly in the experience of the literature. If these principles are not followed, the acting will probably lack conviction and will not improve over time.

For readers, list the principles on the board or a chart and continually refer to them throughout any lesson. If students get off track, it is usually because they are not following one or more of the principles.

Belief

Tell students that believing or fully pretending to be the parts they are playing is essential. The more they are able and willing to believe that they are inside the shoes of a character or the fur, feathers, or skin of an animal, the more dynamic and involving the experience will be. For example, if a student plays a perky rabbit, he or she must pretend to get inside the soft fur of that animal and actually *be* a rabbit with long leaping legs, a wiggling nose, and alert eyes and ears. If someone plays a tortoise, the student must imagine he or she is covered by a thick, protective shell, plodding slowly on stubby legs and claws, head wagging from side to side.

To inspire belief:

- Discuss with students the need to believe in the parts they are playing to make the drama seem real. For an example, refer to the film, *The Wizard of Oz*, pointing out how 17-year-old Judy Garland pretended to be a little girl, and how other actors became a wicked witch, a man of tin, a cowardly lion, and a man of straw.
- Show pictures of the animal or characters students will play.

- Model belief. For example when reading, "a beautiful black crow was flying in the sun," flap your wings and look crow-like. Great skill is unnecessary; you just need enthusiasm. The purpose of modeling is not to make students copy you, but only to stimulate their imaginations and to show the effort that is required.
- Reinforce students' believable acting each time they do a Becoming the Character activity or act out a fable wholeheartedly. Point out the students who are putting effort and imagination into becoming a fierce wind, a hungry dog, a tall pitcher, or a swaying palm tree.
- When an acting assignment is evaluated, ask students to recall which actors seemed to believe the parts they were playing, and what they did that made it seem real.

Control

A most legitimate teacher concern is that students will get out of control when acting. Indeed, drama requires the expression of strong actions and feelings, but it must be done with control. Control gives the drama artistry and purpose.

To help instill and maintain control:

- Discuss the need to exercise control to make the drama artistic and worthwhile. For older students, explain how theatre and film actors use controlled, stylized actions that have been practiced and sometimes choreographed when they fight, leap, push, and carry out other aggressive actions.
- Use the "freeze" command during exuberant actions or whenever the actions might get out of control. For example, say, "Freeze!" when students are growling, running, clawing, leaping, or performing other active emotional scenes. Comment on their "frozen pictures."
- Slow down your own speech, and use a low calm voice to slow down students' action. This is a particularly effective control technique to keep the drama from getting too emotional and exuberant.
- Have students act out in place all the traveling actions, such as running, scurrying, or trotting, in the Becoming the Character warm-ups.
- Show students how to use slow motion or stylized movement for running, leaping, fighting, pushing, or other aggressive actions.
- Have students practice doing voiceless screams or silent roars to capture the expression and feeling with the face and body but with no noise.
- Use a control device, such as a bell, or the commands "action" to begin acting and "freeze" to end it. For example, say, "When I ring the bell, go into character and flap your wings like a crow. When I ring again, go out of character, stop acting, and freeze."
- Praise those using good control, emphasizing how artistic it is.
- Use peer evaluation to point out times when control was good or what students might do to exercise more control.
- End dramatizations with a "quieting activity"; for example, have the character go to sleep.

Voice and Movement

Voice and Movement means using different kinds of voices and body movements and gestures to portray different characters and their feelings. These are the basic tools with which actors portray their parts. For example, a lion would use a deep, powerful voice and move with regal, forceful actions. A mouse, in contrast, would use a small voice and use quick, light, quivering motions.

To teach voice and movement:

- Show pictures of real animals that match the animal characters in the story to help students experience the essence of the characters.
- Have students practice using the voice and movements of two contrasting characters. For example, say "Go away," first as a fierce lion, and then as a frightened mouse.
- Use the Enacting Moments from the Story exercises to strengthen student understanding of using voice and movement to show the characters and their feelings.
- Encourage students to stand on two feet to play animals, as they are portraying both an animal and a character, and can maneuver much better. (Preschoolers may feel more comfortable crawling; allow them to do so.)
- After a fable has been dramatized, evaluate the story, asking students what the actors did with their voices and movement to show they were the characters they were playing.

Children from preschool to grade two do not require a lengthy description of these principles. Younger children need only to be told to make believe, to use control, and to show the characters' feelings with their voices and bodies.

Students in grade three and above benefit greatly from knowing and focusing on these acting concepts that will enrich and improve their acting.

CHAPTER TWO

The Mechanics

This chapter contains tips on how to set up the classroom and teach the lesson to inspire the best acting from students. It also explains how to heighten the drama with sound effects, costumes, and fabric for scenery.

Techniques to Inspire Good Acting

Visual Aids

Pictures stimulate the imagination. Examining pictures of the characters helps students to become the characters. Students are able to project into the picture and identify with their characters' feelings and attitudes, focusing on the characters, rather than on themselves.

To become an animal character, it helps to study pictures of both the real animals and the animals as they appear as characters in the story.

For example, a color photo of a lion helps students to visualize the texture of its fur, the look in its eye, the majesty of its mane, and the power of its graceful body. Having this mental image helps a student become a lion. A picture from the story of the lion clawing at the net or overpowering the mouse helps a student identify with and participate in the dramatic action.

The fables in this book have pictures of the characters in action. Each picture has a dramatic caption question or two asking students to re-create the action or feelings of the characters or to tell what they might be saying or thinking. You may also want to use illustrations from the many different versions of Aesop's fables cited in the bibliography to stimulate characterization. "Zoo Books" (see bibliography) and science or nature picture books focusing on individual animals are also good sources of pictures to help students become the real animals.

Reading Aloud and Storytelling Techniques

Narrators — both teachers and students — can inspire and involve the actors and audience by practicing these techniques:

- Speak slowly and clearly.
- Use your voice to make words sound like what they describe. For example, say, "big," making your voice sound as if it is really big. Say, "tiny," making it

sound small. Say "hot," sounding as if something is boiling hot, or "icy," as if it is freezing cold. This technique makes the language sensual and alive. It is also an excellent way to teach the excitement and meaning of language to limited and nonnative English speakers.

- Use big, clear gestures to make the literature physical and alive. For example, round, flowing motions depict graceful, loving feelings. Jagged, sharp motions indicate unpleasant characters and actions. Hand gestures—pointing, pleading, caressing — make the language and its meaning spring to life.
- Experience the sensual images as you read. For example, picture in your mind's eye a lake shimmering in the sunlight; feel the dazzling sun in your eyes; see and hear the palm tree's big leaves swaying back and forth in the wind. Experiencing these images will help color your voice and make the images come alive.
- Create a different voice and stance for each character. For example, a raucous voice and bouncy movements might depict a crow; a warm soothing voice and slow wing flapping could be a dove.

Student Reflection

After each dramatization, students benefit from telling what they liked doing best or enjoyed most in the drama. This discussion honors each individual's feelings. It also allows students a chance to examine, articulate, and share their personal reactions to what can be a moving and meaningful experience.

Reflection can also give the teacher unexpected insights into students. For example, an aggressive student sometimes best likes the part when the lion and mouse become friends, and a shy child may prefer the moment when the hunters net the lion. Drama gives each person the opportunity to experience and share aspects of themselves that may be unrecognized or hidden.

A simple way to have students reflect is to ask them what they enjoyed doing most or liked best about the fable, and why, and then to draw or write about this favorite part.

Peer Evaluation

Peer evaluation is essential for students in grades three and above to teach them what makes good drama and to challenge them to develop their acting and drama and theatre skills. Without evaluation, students' acting probably will not improve and may even deteriorate. They will not know what to do or focus on to improve.

Peer evaluation is inappropriate for grades two and below. Young students need to dramatize only to develop, enhance, and enjoy the power of their imaginations. They should, however, be supported and encouraged to believe in the parts they are playing, to use control, and to express actions and feelings through voice and movement. For older students, the concept of developing their acting skills often is what makes the experience most rewarding.

Older students observing in the audience should view each peer performance with two goals. First, they should watch to see which actors act their parts believably and what these actors do to make their parts effective and believable. Second, observers should note what might be changed next time to improve or enhance the performance.

Students need guidance to know how to evaluate effectively. Comments must be specific. For example, saying, "She was a good lion," is too vague. Students must pinpoint what the actor specifically did to create "a good lion." For example, what did she do with her arms and hands to look like a big cat padding through the jungle? What did she do with her voice to sound lion-like? Have students try to make positive and specific comments on each player who has tried to play the part sincerely.

Comments on improving might entail finding moments in which the performance might have been made more dramatic or more believable. For example, what else might a boy playing the lion have done to show that he was becoming increasingly upset when he couldn't get out of the net? What else might the hunters have done to show how frightened they were when the lion sprang at them?

Discuss sound effects, too. What effects enhanced the action and helped the actors play their parts? Was the drum beat for the lion powerful and strong? Was the skittering sound of the mouse crisp and emphatic? Might other effects be added?

It takes training to articulate what was specifically done and what might be added. It also takes time. Evaluation, though, is exhilarating and creative. Students are learning what actors and directors do to produce an exciting, believable play, and they are learning to create and produce one themselves.

Evaluation also gives the audience an important active role that will lead to more involvement in the drama. It develops critical thinking and oral language skills and trains students in aesthetic judgment. Students can watch TV dramas and films with more critical awareness and discuss how actors played their parts or how sound effects were made or used.

Try to evaluate immediately after each performance. When this is done, students become invested in the creative process and making it work. For example, the behavior of a student who uses the drama not to play the role, but to show off can be redirected by having students discuss whether these actions really portrayed the character in the story. Students' unique interpretations of the characters and objects come out in their playing and in their suggestions during the evaluation period.

Reinforcing and Developing Imagination

A central goal of story dramatization is to reinforce, encourage, and develop students' imaginative powers. Three techniques foster and encourage this process.

The first technique is continual reinforcement of committed, believable playing. The second is the teacher's enthusiastic response, either through direct participation or by showing enthusiasm for student participation. The third and most important technique is to listen to and foster students' creative ideas.

To reinforce different interpretations during the Becoming the Character warm-ups, you might say such things as, "I see some palm trees with huge leaves swaying; I see others that are bending over in a heavy wind; I hear a few trees whistling in the wind." This shows your involvement and enthusiasm for their creativity.

Naturally, the more students' ideas are used, the better the reinforcement. For example, a student might suggest that the ant go underneath the blue fabric of the brook to show that she is drowning. Someone else might suggest that the trapper hop up and down in a circle to show how hard the ant bit him.

Even if an idea is impractical, such as painting a long piece of paper blue for the brook, an appreciation of the idea and an explanation why it might be too time-consuming is valuable. Students benefit from knowing that art consists of thinking and considering many ideas, using some and not others.

Creating a Theater in Your Classroom

Locating Your Classroom Stage
The traditional classroom makes a good theater, with the student desks serving as the audience area and the front of the room serving as the stage. Designated areas on each side of the stage can be "off stage," where actors wait to enter to play their parts. Areas around the room's perimeter can be used to stage certain scenes, and the aisles make good woodland paths or streets where characters can enter or exit.

For example, in "The Hare and the Tortoise," the front of the room might be the central forest area where the race begins and ends. The race might take place around the edge of the room, with the hare sleeping in a designated place along the way. In "The Wind and the Sun," the wind might blow in from the back of the class, continue down an aisle, and exit up another aisle.

Another way to stage a play is theater in the round, with both audience and actors sitting around a circle, using the center as the stage. Characters step into the center to act, and sit down when their parts are over.

A circle lets everyone see everything and unites the group. It also allows those seated, if desired, to play group parts, such as the shimmering lake or swaying palm trees, and to create sound effects. Theater in the round works particularly well for kindergarten through grade two.

Placing Imaginary Scenery
Classroom creative dramatics relies on students using their imaginations to become the scenery to pretend through pantomime, or to use pieces of fabric for scenery. Students playing the scenery must know exactly where to go, so that each piece of scenery has a definite place.

Locate scenery in easy-to-remember places. For example, put the berry bush in front of Jose's desk or the lake in front of the chalkboard, and review these locations two or three times.

Place the scenery and actors in separate, distinct locations so that the stage will not be crowded or cluttered and the layout will be artistic and clear.

Another method of scenery placement is to make signs on 5-by-7-inch cards with the names of the scenic pieces written on them such as "lake," "tree," or "bush," and put them on the floor where these actors should stand.

Enhancing the Drama

Sound Effects

Students enjoy making sound effects with their voices and commercial or make-shift rhythm instruments. Older or shy students often become involved in the the drama by creating sound effects. Students like to explore what might be used to create a special effect.

Creating sound effects develops listening skills, teaches an important theatrical technique, heightens and enhances the action, and makes the drama seem more real. Indeed, students might read a fable and create only the sound effects to go with it in a kind of radio theatre.

The human voice is a most versatile instrument. Young people often have an amazing capacity for creating authentic sound effects vocally. There is something liberating in using the lips, teeth, tongue, and voice in this sensual way. Students will spontaneously make lively vocal imitations of whistling palm trees, tweeting birds, bubbling brooks, and cawing crows. One vocal technique is repeating words to mean what they say. For example, say, "hop, hop, hop," "bubble, bubble, bubble," or "paw, paw, paw," to sound like these actions. This is an excellent technique to make language fun and meaningful for LEP students.

Rhythm instruments enchant students and add a theatrical touch. Many rhythm instruments, such as triangles and woodblocks, are surprisingly inexpensive. Sets of several different instruments can be purchased from music education companies. It is best to buy good quality, not "toy" instruments, for sound and durability.

Good instruments for creating many different effects include six-inch triangles, drums, tambourines, a wood block with a mallet, sandpaper blocks, guiros, rhythm sticks, maracas (or other rattles or shakers), castanets on a handle, and bells of various kinds. These instruments come from different cultures, and it is worthwhile to discuss their origin and use in these cultures. All these instruments should be played with a certain emphasis to heighten and enhance the action and to make it clear and dramatic. They can be struck, tapped, rubbed, stroked, or shaken to create different effects. Let students have fun experimenting.

For example, beating a drum firmly and steadily creates strong, powerful actions, such as a lion padding. Tapping the drum lightly with fingertips creates a sound like a little animal scurrying or raindrops. Scraping fingers on the drum head creates a spooky, suspenseful atmosphere. Tap a triangle on the outside or run the beater all around the inside for entirely different effects.

A piano is versatile. Continuously hit a low note or high note to create animals' movements. Tinkle two high notes, or run fingers along several notes for magical effects. Press down hard with the arm on a section of low notes to create a storm or a thundering giant. In these fables, for example, repeat one or two high notes for a bird hopping; play a group of low notes heavily for the howling wind; strike quick notes for the hare hopping; and slow, low notes for the tortoise plodding. Instruments made quickly from objects found around the house or outdoors are imaginative and can be as effective as the commercial versions.

For example, tightly sealed containers full of pebbles or beans sound different, depending on how many pebbles are inside. Different types of drinking glasses, or the same type with different levels of water can be tapped with a spoon. Tapping a pencil on a desk with just the right emphasis and speed sounds like tapping a drum lightly. Rattling a piece of paper sounds like a storm.

Some other effective homemade instruments are an oatmeal box for a drum and wooden dowels for rhythm sticks. Students can also use objects in the room or experiment with striking, scraping, tapping, or hitting various objects or pieces of furniture. They can look at home to find items that will create interesting effects.

Brainstorming helps. Ask, for example, "What might be used to create a furious wind storm?" "What might we do to create a sound for the sun beaming down?"

A good method to stimulate involvement and creativity is to display instruments on a table and let students suggest which instrument to use for which effect. Play the instruments to let students hear the different sounds and to decide whether an instrument sounds right for the desired effect.

To prevent students from monopolizing instruments when they are working in groups, let them decide which instruments to use for different parts, but permit playing only during practice and performance.

Costumes and Scenery

Costumes that merely suggest characters, and fabric used for scenery backdrops create theatricality. To keep the focus on the development of the imagination, the stress should be on simplicity.

Fabrics, hats, and other simple costumes enchant all ages. They are especially effective with nonnative or limited-English speakers who can understand and enjoy the story and the action with these visual aids.

Even a sign with the character's name or a picture hanging around the neck inspires and helps some students to become their roles.

Simple costumes can be found in thrift stores, garage sales, and among your own throwaways. Check the yellow pages under *costumes* or *party* for stores that have inexpensive paper crowns, hats, and interesting props.

The simpler the costumes, the more students use their own ingenuity to make them work. For example, one teacher in a workshop tied a big piece of yellow nylon netting fabric around her head to create a most effective lion's mane.

In this regard, pieces of fabric not sewn in any way are sometimes best. Inexpensive fabric remnants can be draped over the shoulders and tied to create bird wings, cloaks, or tree leaves. Fabric might also be tied around the waist or head and used in many creative ways.

It is fun to keep a box of costumes and fabrics in the classroom. The same pieces can be used over and over again, because they need not represent exactly a particular character but may just suggest an attribute.

For example, a fox might wear a jaunty red hat or visor. A stork might don a white piece of material or shawl around the shoulders. (Students could decorate the costume box in a collage with drawings of their favorite characters.)

Suggested costume pieces for your box:

- Hats, particularly baseball caps of various colors. These work well for animal characters. The bill can become a bird's beak or an animal's snout. Students can turn the cap around for a tortoise or other snoutless creature. Furry hats are also good for animals. (Use hat liners for health reasons.)
- Remnants or strips of material for capes, headdresses, sashes, and other creative uses.
- Gloves and mittens. Purple, bright blue, or red gloves can become dangling grapes, berries, or flowers; black ones can be the legs of an insect; and mittens can be animal paws.
- Shawls or big scarves, draped around the body to create different effects. Scarves can also be rippled, flapped, or swirled to create scenic effects.

Here are a few simple homemade costumes:

- Tagboard or cardboard headbands with construction paper ears or beaks (perhaps backed by tagboard for durability) and stapled on for animal headpieces.
- No-sew animal ears cut out of felt and stapled to an elastic band that is knotted in the back.
- A white paper-cup beak with an elastic band stapled onto the two sides of the cup and worn around the head.

As mentioned, fabrics of different textures and colors also create wonderful scenic effects. These work well for Aesop's fables, because for the ancient Greeks (and many other early cultures, such as the Native Americans) the whole world was alive, animated, and full of wonder.

Standard colors to use are blue for bodies of water, green for trees, white netting for mystical effects, brown for earth, yellow for the sun, and black or gray for ominous effects. For example, ripple blue or aqua material to represent a river, a brook, or a lake; flap black shiny material to create an evil wind; swirl white netting for clouds.

CHAPTER THREE

How to Dramatize the Stories in This Book

Overview

The stories in this book were adapted for use with the narrative-mime approach to dramatize literature. Sentences are written with actions to do and feelings to show. Sensual images stimulate students to become the characters fully.

To dramatize a story, a narrator reads the story, pausing at the end of each sentence to give the players time to pantomime the actions, show the characters' feelings, and ad-lib or repeat dialogue. Students can also make sound effects with voice, body, or rhythm instruments. They play both the characters and the inanimate objects.

For example, in "The Lion and the Mouse," when the narrator reads, "Once a beautiful golden lion came padding through the jungle," the students become the lion and pad along. When the narrator reads, "He saw a shimmering lake," students become the lake with their arms, hands, and bodies.

When the narrator reads, "The lion said, 'I'm King of the Jungle,'" the lion repeats the dialogue in a lion-like voice. Or the narrator might pause and let the lion make up something appropriate to say, such as "I'm great," or "I'm the strongest animal in the world."

Sound effects can accompany the action, such as slapping the thighs or beating a desk or drum to simulate the lion padding. Lightly ringing bells or saying, "shimmer, shimmer, shimmer" could sound like a shimmering lake. Simple costumes can be added, such as tagboard ears or yellow mittens for the lion, red gloves for a berry bush, or fabric for scenery, such as a piece of blue cloth for the lake.

Narrative mime can be done with everyone acting every part of the story at the same time as the teacher reads. Or it can be done as a play, with a narrator reading and individuals cast in each role. In this case, for example, one student would play the lion; another, the mouse; and others, the lake and the berry bush.

The following methods describe two ways to dramatize these stories, with some variations. Methods for primary and upper grades are described. The chapter also explains two ways to dramatize the fables in cooperative groups for younger and older students.

All methods include Becoming the Character acting warm-ups to help students get into character and learn how to dramatize. The following section, however, describes only the methods themselves. For a specific example of an introductory lesson in literature dramatization, see Chapter 4. It describes in detail "The Lion and the Mouse," a story dramatized as a first lesson for all students through grade six.

Everybody Plays All the Parts

Participants: Preschool through grade two and LEP students.

Benefits: Limited English speakers learn language and literature simultaneously. Young students enjoy experiencing every part of the literature.

Description: The teacher reads the story, and all the students act every character and object in the story with the teacher. They might also make sound effects with their voice, bodies, or desks.

Procedure: The teacher reads the story and pauses at the end of each sentence to perform the actions described with the students. For example (using "The Wind and the Sun"), the teacher reads, "Once the big bully wind came along, and he blew three times: Woosh, woosh, woosh." The teacher and students become the wind, puffing up their cheeks and using bully voices, saying, "Woosh, woosh, woosh." Next the teacher reads, "He saw the gentle sun shining three times: Shine, shine, shine." The teacher and students become the sun, saying gently, "Shine, shine, shine." They might hold up their hands and wiggle their fingers to portray the sun. (The teacher and students can decide exactly how to portray the parts described.)

This method has two simple variations.

Variation One: Everybody Plays the Major Character

Participants: Preschool through grade two and LEP students.

Benefits: Students experience the conflicts and situation of the major character of the story throughout.

Description: This variation is similar to the above method, in that the teacher reads and students act along. However, in this variation, students play only the central character and pretend through pantomime that the objects in the story are there. This method is suitable for stories with one major character involved in action throughout the story, such as the crow in "The Crow and the Pitcher" or the dog in "The Dog and His Reflection."

Procedure: The teacher reads the story, and everyone plays only the major character (for example, the crow), pretending that the objects (for example, the hot sun and the pitcher) are there.

Variation Two: Everybody Plays Either of Two Major Characters

Participants: Kindergarten through grade two and LEP students.

Benefits: Students experience one of the major characters and interact with students playing the other major character.

Description: For stories with two major characters, such as "The Wind and the Sun," "The Hare and the Tortoise," or "The Ant and the Dove," the class is divided in half. One half is assigned to play one of the major characters (for example, the wind) and the other half of the class, the other major character (for example, the sun). The teacher, an aide, or perhaps a designated student might play the small parts, such as the people buttoning up their coats in "The Wind and the Sun" or the badger who starts the race in "The Hare and the Tortoise."

Procedure: The teacher assigns half of the class one of the major roles to play and assigns the other half the other major role. Each group is instructed to act only its part. For example, when the teacher reads, "Once the big bully wind came along and blew three times," the group playing the wind does this. Then when the narrator reads, "He saw the gentle sun shining three times: "Shine, shine, shine," the group playing the sun says and does this. (The roles could be reversed later to let all students experience both roles.)

Dramatizing Fables as Plays

Participants: Grades one and above and LEP students. This method is particularly effective with students grade three and above as they learn serious acting methods.

Benefits: Students act and also observe the story as a live play. LEP students visualize and experience the story completely (particularly when simple costumes and rhythm instruments are added).

Description: This method makes the stories into playlets, with individual students cast in each role. The narrator (the teacher or an older student) reads the story and students step forward and dramatize their parts when they occur. (Nonreaders might narrate by telling the story, rather than reading it.) A crew is also chosen to make sound effects to accompany the action. Simple costumes might be added for the characters, with pieces of fabric to simulate the scenery.

Procedure: The teacher chooses students to play each character and object and selects others to make sound effects. (A list of characters and sound effects suggestions are given with each fable.) The teacher determines where to have the classroom "stage" (possibly the reading circle area) and points out where those playing scenery, such as the lake, should stand. The teacher explains that he or she will narrate the story, and students will dramatize their parts when they come up.

The teacher reviews the procedure. For example, the teacher might say, "When I read, 'A great big lion came padding along,' what will the lion do? When I read, 'A lake was shimmering,' who comes onto the stage, and what will that person do?"

Discuss how to ad-lib dialogue. Say, for example, "When I read, 'The lion thought he was great, and said...,' what might the lion actor say?" Let students offer several suggestions. (LEP students and the youngest students will probably just repeat the dialogue that the narrator reads.)

For grades three and above, the teacher instructs students in the audience to watch and to be ready to evaluate those who acted their parts believably and the sound effects that enhanced the action. The audience should also tell what might be added to improve or strengthen future creative dramatics.

To begin and end, it helps to say, "Curtain" to create focus and theatricality. For example, saying, "Curtain" in the beginning means that the audience should focus on the stage, because the curtain is going up, and the play will begin. "Curtain" at the end means that the curtain is coming down, and the play is over. Then the evaluation can begin.

Dramatizing Fables in Cooperative Groups

Of all drama activities, students most enjoy acting on their own in cooperative groups. Understandably, students are highly motivated because they can try out their own ideas and have the excitement of performing in a play. This builds confidence and a feeling of joy. It also makes the drama and the literature their own.

The following subsections describe two methods of cooperative acting—one for younger students and one for older students.

Beginning Cooperative Groups

Participants: Kindergarten through grade three.

Benefits: Teamwork; all students play a major part.

Description: The teacher reads the story, and student groups go to various areas of the room to act the story while the teacher reads.

Procedure: The teacher picks one fable for all groups to act. He or she divides the students into groups, giving each group the number of people needed to act the story (using the character list given with each fable). The teacher assigns each group member a role in the fable, giving those with minor roles more than one part.

For example, "The Ant and the Dove" has six roles. There are two main characters, the ant and the dove; and several minor ones — the bubbling brook, the water reed, the leaf, and the bird trapper. There could be four students in each group — two students to play the main characters and two others to divide up all the minor parts. The second two could play these minor roles together.

To perform, groups go to various areas in the room. The teacher says, "Curtain" and narrates the story while all groups act the story at the same time. At the end, the teacher says, "Curtain," and all the players take a bow and go to their seats. (It helps to have an aide or older student to help oversee the groups.) After playing the story, roles might be reversed so that students have opportunities to play other parts.

Advanced Cooperative Groups

Participants: Grades three and above and those able to read the stories. (Nonreaders could also use this method by telling the story.)

Benefits: This method develops teamwork and nurtures creativity. It trains students to be artistic directors, making the artistic decisions themselves.

Description: This method is similar to the Dramatizing Fables As Plays method. This time, however, students act the story, narrate it and do all the acting warm-ups and follow-ups on their own in groups. Then they perform their dramatization for the class. This method will be most successful if the teacher first does a model lesson of the Dramatizing the Story as a Play method with the whole class so that they will know what to do in their groups.

Materials Needed: One copy of the story and related activities for the narrator in each group.

Procedure: The teacher decides whether to have all groups act the same fable or to give each group a different fable. She or he makes one copy of the fable for each narrator. The teacher puts students into appropriate groups. The groups are then sent to various areas in the room to practice their dramatizations.

Students decide who will play the narrator, the characters, and those who make sound effects. Those playing small parts might play more than one part and make sound effects, too. Groups might choose more than one narrator. Then they practice dramatizing the story.

The narrator reads the Becoming the Character and Re-enacting Moments from the Story activities, for students to do. In this method, students may do these activities after they act the story to deepen and strengthen characterization.

The groups should have about fifteen minutes to practice. A brief time focuses creativity and interest. Students then reassemble and present their plays to each other. After each presentation, the audience evaluates it, discussing who played their parts believably, what they did to make them believable, and what might be added next time to improve the acting.

Replaying: After the evaluation, have the groups perform the story again, using suggestions given by peers and the teacher and their own new ideas. Some might bring in costumes and present their playlets to other classes.

Follow-ups: Have students discuss the critical-thinking questions in their groups. One student may ask the questions or students may take turns. The art follow-up of illustrating different fables in a mural (discussed in Chapter 9) might also be done in groups.

CHAPTER FOUR

A Model Lesson: The Lion and the Mouse

The following material is a model for teaching literature dramatization. This introductory lesson, "The Lion and the Mouse," has been used successfully with mainstream, gifted, and LEP students from preschool to grade six.

The lesson is only a model, of course, and you will want to add or eliminate activities as you see fit. For example, you might decide to do only some of the Becoming the Character or Re-enacting Moments from the Story activities, or you might do a few of them as an alternative to performing the whole story.

"The Lion and the Mouse" was chosen as a first lesson because the characters are distinct and are good models to teach the process of becoming different types of characters. The activities given here are the same as those in "The Lion and the Mouse" lesson that appears in Chapter 6 of this book. They are repeated here with details of classroom procedure.

Dramatizing a story might be done in one day or over several days. For example, some teachers might want just to act the story as written and do no warm-ups. Other teachers, however, might want to spread the lesson over several days, introducing Aesop and his fables one day, doing the Becoming the Character warm-ups the second day; acting out the whole fable the third day; and writing, discussing, or doing art or other activities on a fourth or fifth day. There is no one right way to proceed.

"The Lion and the Mouse"

Materials
The background information on Aesop and his fables in this book (see Chapter 5)
"The Lion and the Mouse" story in this book
Pictures of the lion and mouse characters from this book
Bell or other control device
Pictures of real lions and mice (optional)
Other Aesop's fables picture books with "The Lion and the Mouse" (optional)

Introducing the Overall Goal
Procedure: Tell students that they will become the characters in the Aesop's fable, "The Lion and the Mouse," and will dramatize the story.

Depending on age level and English-speaking ability, discuss Aesop and the fable form. Show pictures of the lion and mouse characters from this book and other books. Read the story. For LEP students, tell the story in their native language if possible.

Discussing the Three Principles of Good Acting

Procedure: Explain that students need to follow three principles of good acting. For students in grades two and below, just say that there are three things they need to do to play the story well. (The concept of "acting" is irrelevant to those below grade three.) Eliminate this step and all other didactic discussion activities with non-English speakers. They will learn the principles through demonstration and practice.

For those able to read, list the principles on a chart or on the chalkboard:

Believing
Believe that you are the part you are playing.

Control
Exercise control over your actions and emotions.

Voice and Movement
Use voice and movement expressively to portray different characters.

For grades three and above, ask what it means to say that actors must believe they are the parts they are playing to make the drama and the characters seem real. Use the film *The Wizard of Oz* as an example.

Discussing Lions to Prepare to Become One

Procedure: Show pictures of real lions. Ask how a lion is different from a person. Usual responses are: lions walk on four legs, are covered with fur, have manes and sharp teeth, eat meat, are powerful, and roar.

Introducing the Bell

Procedure: Introduce the use of the bell for control. Show students the bell and tell them that they may start acting when you ring the bell and must stop acting when you ring it again. Use this signal for all the Becoming the Character activities. For LEP students, point to yourself and the bell and pretend to ring it. (For these students the teacher's modeling of the following Becoming the Character activities is essential.)

Becoming Lions

Procedure: Read each of the following suggestions for action, or say them in your own words, ringing the bell for action to begin and ringing it again to stop.

- You're asleep among the soft, gently waving grasses. Get up and stretch your beautiful, long, golden legs and paws and pad quietly through the jungle.
- Reach your front paws high into the air, extend your claws, and sharpen them on a tree trunk.
- Paw along looking for food. See juicy red meat on the ground, pounce on it with your paws, rip into it, chew, and swallow. Take several bites and then toss it to the side.
- You're thirsty. See a lake. Paw up to it and lap, lap, lap the cool water with your big, long, rough lion tongue. Roar with pleasure. Freeze.
- Stand up to a mighty height, reach up a paw and say in a royal voice, "I'm King of the Jungle." Freeze, showing how mighty you are.
- You're tired. Stretch out your beautiful, long lion body, shake your mane, and fall fast asleep.

Reinforcing Belief with the Lion

Procedure: To reinforcing believable acting, praise those believing. Point out specifics you observed. For example, perhaps mention some students looking as if they had long, golden, furry legs and pawing quietly like big quiet cats, those showing sharp teeth and ripping into the meat, or those speaking majestically like royal lions. For LEP students, point to or smile at active participants.

Discussing Control

Procedure: For grades three and above, ask what it means to say that actors, dancers, or baseball players must have control over their movements and emotions to make their performances good.

Point out that even if a character is angry and fights, this must be done in a controlled, stylized way. Explain how actors take classes in controlled stage combat. Tell students in grades two and below that they need to have control to make a good play. Eliminate the discussion for LEP students, and let the following techniques in the exercises demonstrate control.

Practicing Control: Becoming the Mouse

Procedure: Show pictures of real mice. Ask how mice are different from lions. For LEP students, point to pictures of mice eating, hiding in a hole, and showing facial features. Ask students to act like the animals in these pictures at their desks.

Usual responses: Mice are tiny and hide in holes. Their noses quiver, and they have big ears and eyes to protect themselves from enemies. Their teeth are blunt, and they eat berries and nuts. They squeak.

Tell students to perform the following actions when you ring the bell.

- You are tucked up tight in your mouse hole. Poke your head out and look around for enemies. Freeze!
- Sniff all around and turn your ears and eyes around this way and that. Pop out of your mouse hole and scurry lightly in place.

- See a berry bush. Pluck one berry and nibble it. Pluck a second berry a little higher on the bush and nibble it, and then a third berry almost above your reach. All the time keep sniffing and looking around.
- See a puddle and lick the water with your rough little mouse tongue. Freeze!
- Look up and see a big owl hovering above. Freeze in fear. Squeak and quiver with fear.
- Scurry back and squeeze deep into your mouse hole. Your heart is going pat, pat, pat. Show me with your hand how it's going. Now it's going slower. Show me with your hand in slow motion that it's patting slower.
- Poke your head out of the hole to see if owl has gone. Ah, he has. Pull your self in tight and go to sleep. ("Going to Sleep" is a good control technique to use to conclude any acting activity, bringing it to a quiet, satisfying ending.)

Reinforcing Control

Procedure: Point out specifics of good control you saw. For example, demonstrate how students all moved quietly and lightly in place and "froze" together.

Discussing Voice and Movement

Procedure: Ask what it means to use voices and bodies to show character roles. For grades three and above, explain that voice and movement are the tools actors use, the most important way to show what kinds of characters they are playing and what they are like.

For younger students and LEP students, demonstrate how they can use their voices and bodies. For example, make your body big and say, "Go away" as a giant. Then make it tiny and say, "Go away" as an ant.

Practicing Voice and Movement

Procedure: Have students become the hunters. Ask why hunters must be quiet and cautious to capture prey. Explain the following scenario and tell students that when you ring the bell, they should do the following four things. For LEP students, demonstrate what to do. (This exercise also functions as a control exercise.)

- First you'll be hunters sneaking through tall brush. Sneak in place. Push back the heavy brush with your arms.
- Second, you'll see the lion sleeping and you'll stop and point.
- Next you'll all pick up a heavy net, and on the count of three, toss it together over the lion to capture him.
- Last you'll sneak back through the brush to to get a truck to take the lion away. Again, sneak in place.

Ring the bell and coach students through this. Have LEP students do it with you. This is a favorite warm-up. Students like the excitement of the scene. They enjoy working together and doing the actions with control.

Again, reinforce the effectiveness of the control and how good it looked when all the students worked together. This exercise also functions as a control exercise.

Becoming the Scenery

Procedure: Explain that there are objects in the fable, and it is fun and creative to dramatize them. Explain too that for the ancient Greeks and other ancient peoples, the whole world was alive and animate. Demonstrate how to become the shimmering lake, the swaying palm tree, and the berry bush, with big plump berries for the mouse to eat; then let students dramatize each object in turn.

Reinforcing Objects

Procedure: After students have become each object, express delight at the variety of interpretations, and point out how every student used his or her own imagination.

Students are now ready to dramatize the story, using one of the methods described in Chapter 2.

After acting, students might work on one or more of the drama, critical-thinking, research, or art follow-ups given with the story.

CHAPTER FIVE

Aesop and His Fables: Dramatizing the Stories

Background

Ever since prehistoric days, people who lived close to deer, wolves, and other animals have put animals into their stories. But it was the Greeks, and most notably Aesop, who made the fable what it is today — a short, witty, action-packed story with animals who act like people and teach people important lessons.

No one is sure whether Aesop existed, but most people believe that he did. He may have been a black slave born on the Island of Samos in Greece or in Phrygia in the 6th century B.C. Deformed and misshapen, he was supposedly also born unable to speak.

According to legend, the Greek Muses gave Aesop speech for his kindness in helping a priestess who had lost her way. Later his philosopher master freed him from slavery, because Aesop's gifts of wit, wisdom, and speech were so great that the master felt inferior to him.

Although people may have laughed at Aesop's appearance, they laughed more at his funny, wise fables. His storytelling became so popular that he was in demand in courts throughout Greece. Aesop had truly developed the special gifts given to him.

According to many versions of the story, however, Aesop's truths disturbed some people so much that later they placed a golden goblet among his belongings, making it look as if he had stolen it. Aesop was thrown from a cliff in Delphi and killed on this false charge.

No one has ever killed the spirit of Aesop, though. His fables have lasted more than 2,500 years, longer than almost any other literature. The fables have been translated into almost every language in the world and have been read and told by all races and countries. The characters and situations in the stories are as familiar as household words in the daily conversation of all countries.

No one is certain why Aesop told his fables, but many were probably created to criticize the Greek government. The people, particularly slaves, couldn't speak out against unfair or cruel leaders. Aesop probably created his bossy lion, tricky fox, and boastful hare to depict certain government officials. No one could condemn Aesop for criticizing people, though, because it was the animals in the stories who behaved badly.

Animals are a wonderful vehicle for showing the good and bad qualities of people. Animals are entirely natural and do not try to disguise who they are. Over time, certain animals have been associated with certain traits — the sly fox, the peace-loving dove, the kingly lion, and the meek mouse. Thus, when these animals appear in stories, we know how they are supposed to act, and we look forward to them acting that way.

Both children and adults enjoy Aesop's fables. More writers and illustrators have drawn and adapted his fables than almost any other literature. (Only the Bible has been illustrated more.) Every illustrator and adapter's version differs, depending on the viewpoint of the artists, their artistic style, and the times in which they lived.

Writers usually add morals or lessons to the fables. It is unlikely, however, that Aesop ever did so. As is true of most great artists, he probably left the lesson up to the listeners to discover for themselves. Interestingly, writers have sometimes found entirely different lessons or morals in the fables. This is part of Aesop's greatness; his fables contain many different truths in very short stories.

After reading or acting a fable, it is fun to discuss different possible meanings. Students can be like the ancient Greeks, enjoying the fun of these fables while at the same time probing their deep wisdom. Indeed, they may even come up with a new twist.

Critical-Thinking Questions

Use these questions for discussion or written response.

1. What handicaps did Aesop probably face?

2. Why might some people have been cruel to Aesop? What do you think of this kind of person? Explain.

3. How do people feel if someone is cruel to them or tries to put them down? Why do people feel that way?

4. Why do you think Aesop succeeded despite many handicaps?

5. What does it mean to say that Aesop developed his special gift? What gift did Aesop have?

6. What does it mean to say that everyone has one or more special gifts?

7. What do you enjoy most — reading, writing, art, acting, sports, or playing music? Discuss one or two of the things you like doing best with a friend. What part of the activity do you enjoy most? These may be your special gifts to enjoy and develop. Draw and write about one or two of your favorite activities and tell why you like them.

The Lion and the Mouse
by Aesop
adapted by Louise Thistle

Cast of Characters (five or more):
Narrators (one or more)
Lion
Mouse
Lake (two)
Palm tree (one or more)
Berry bush (one or more)
Hunters (up to five)
(The same two students might play the lake, the tree, the bush, and the hunters.)

Sound-Effects Suggestions
Vocal sounds or sounds made with objects: Thump a desk for the sound of the lion padding; tap a desk with pencil for the mouse scurrying; use voice for the shimmering lake; use whistling-wind vocal sound for swaying palm trees; tap a glass with a spoon each time the mouse plucks berries; shake bean-filled containers for hunters sneaking.

Rhythm instruments: Use a drum for the lion padding, a wood block and mallet for the mouse scurrying, bells for the shimmering lake, a triangle for the palm tree swaying and for the mouse plucking each berry, shakers and/or sand blocks for hunters sneaking through brush.

Once a beautiful golden lion came pawing through the jungle. Paw, paw, paw. He thought he was great, and he roared, "I am King of the Jungle." He saw a shimmering lake. Shimmer, shimmer, shimmer. The lion was thirsty. So he padded to the lake and lap, lap, lapped the cool water with his long, rough, lion tongue.

Now he was tired. He saw a swaying palm tree. Sway, sway, sway. The lion padded slowly over to it to go to sleep. But before he stretched out, first he sniffed to the left. Then he sniffed to the right.

Finally he sniffed all around for enemies. Sniffing none, he stretched out his long beautiful lion body, shook his mane, and fell fast asleep.

In the meantime, a little mouse came skittering along. She skittered here. She skittered there. She skittered everywhere.

She was hungry and saw a berry bush. She scurried to the bush and plucked one berry. She nibble, nibble, nibbled the sweet berry. She plucked a second berry and nibble, nibble, nibbled; and a third berry and nibble, nibble, nibbled.

She, too, was thirsty and saw the shimmering lake. She skittered over and lap, lap, lapped the water with her tiny little mouse tongue. She washed the berry juice off her paws. She lifted her paws high up into air and yawned.

Then she saw what looked like a golden hill. She scurried there to lie down. But she accidentally put her paw on the lion's back, and the lion woke up with a "Roar, roar, roar!"

The mouse jumped back and said, "Oh, oh, oh, I'm sorry, your majesty. I didn't mean to disturb you."

But the lion said, "I'm going to eat you up." The mouse bowed and bowed and said, "Oh, no, no, no, don't do that." The lion roared, "Why not?" The mouse hopped up and down, thinking and thinking. Then she said, "Maybe someday I can help you."

The lion threw his head to one side and laughed, "Ha, ha, ha." He threw back his head on the other side and laughed, "Ha, ha, ha." Finally his whole body shook and shook with the greatest laughter of all, "Ha, ha, ha!"

Then he said, "How could a tiny creature like you help a big, important beast like me?"

The mouse said, "Well, you never know."

Then the lion said, "That joke is so funny, I'm going to let you go."

The mouse bowed and bowed to his majesty and scurried off into the jungle. But before she left, she turned and said, "I won't forget my promise."

Dramatizing Aesop's Fables

Now the lion was so tired that he forgot to sniff for enemies. He just stretched out his big lion body and fell fast asleep.

In the meantime, some hunters came sneaking through the tall brush. Sneak, sneak, sneak. They stopped, and one hunter said, "Look at that big golden lion." Another hunter said, "Let's get him with the big net."

So the hunters sneaked back and picked up a big net. Then, saying, "One, two, three," together they tossed the net over the lion. One hunter said, "Let's go get the truck." And they sneaked back again through the brush.

Then the lion woke up, and he felt the net all around him. And he began to roar. First he clawed one side of the net. Then he clawed the other side of the net. Finally he clawed the top of the net. Then he threw his whole body against it and thrashed and roared in fear and alarm.

The little mouse heard the lion and said, "I know that roar." She skittered out from the jungle and said, "I'll help you, your majesty."

First she nibbled one side of the net. Then she nibbled the other side of the net. Then she nibbled the middle. The lion could hear the hunters returning and cried, "Hurry up!" Just then the hunters returned. As they were about to grab the lion, the mouse nibbled the last part of the net, and the lion sprang forth with a mighty roar. The hunters ran into the jungle with mouths open in fear and alarm.

Then the mouse bowed to the king and said, "I was happy to serve you, your majesty."

But the lion raised his paw and said, "You don't have to bow to me. I'm going to bow to you, because you have shown me that the smallest thing can be the most valuable of all." And the lion bowed long and deeply before the mouse.

Then the big lion and the little tiny mouse walked side by side through the jungle, and they were friends forevermore. 🐾

Dramatizing the Story

Becoming the Characters

Show students a picture of each character and discuss its attributes. Refer to the information provided. Then give students the following directions to let them become each character.

Lion Information: Lions have big golden manes and fur, and long tails and bodies. They have strong claws and long, sharp teeth for grabbing prey and ripping into it. They sleep up to 20 hours a day when their stomachs are full. Lions have a roar that can be heard for four miles and are called King of the Jungle.

Becoming Lions

- Stretch out your beautiful long golden legs and paws and paw slowly through the jungle.
- Raise your front legs and paws high into the air, extend your claws, and sharpen them on a tree trunk.
- Paw along looking for food. See a big piece of raw, red meat. Pounce on the meat with your claws. Pick it up in your paws and rip into the tough, red meat with your long, sharp teeth. Take several bites and then toss it aside.

- You're thirsty. Paw to the lake. Put your big head down and lap, lap, lap the cool water with your long, rough, lion tongue.
- Show that you're the great king of the jungle. Stand tall with one paw held high and say in a royal voice, "I am King of the Jungle."
- Now you're tired. Shake your big golden mane. Stretch out your long lion legs. Put your big beautiful head down and fall fast asleep.

Mouse Information: Mice are small and quick with big alert eyes, noses that are always quivering, and big ears to warn them of enemies. They have long blunt front teeth for gnawing berries and nuts, and tiny paws that can pluck and hold things.

Becoming Mice

- Show yourself being tucked in your mouse hole.
- Poke your head out and look to left and right for enemies.
- Sniff all around you.
- Scurry out lightly in place. See a raspberry bush. Pluck one, two, three berries and nibble them. Keep sniffing and looking around.
- Lick water from a puddle.
- Wash berry juice off your paws with your little mouse tongue.

- Look up and see a big owl hovering above. Squeak and quiver in fear. Scurry quickly back to your mouse hole, pull yourself in tight and pant in fear.
- Peek out to see if the owl has gone. Ah, he has. Curl up tight and go to sleep.

Becoming the Hunters

- Sneak through tall brush quietly so as not to awaken the lion.
- Say in a loud whisper, "Look at that big lion."
- With the other hunters, pick up a heavy net, sneak up on the lion, and then on a count of three, toss the net over the lion.
- Make a frozen picture showing (with your body and on your faces) your fear when the lion springs free.

Becoming the Lake, the Palm Tree, and the Berry Bush

- Show a shimmering lake with your hands and body.
- Become a swaying palm tree — first swaying in a light breeze, then in a heavier wind, and finally reaching leaves over to shade the lion.
- Become a berry bush filled with plump berries for the mouse to eat.

Re-enacting Moments from the Story

The Lion

- Show how your face looks when you are awakened by the mouse.
- Laugh "Ha, ha, ha," showing how scornful you are that a mere mouse would think she could help you.
- Say scornfully, "That's the funniest joke I've ever heard."
- Awaken and discover the net around you. Claw one side, claw the other, and finally thrash all around with your whole body.
- Implore the mouse to "hurry up" her nibbling when you hear hunters coming.
- Bow humbly to the mouse and say, "No, you don't have to bow to me. I'm going to bow to you."

The Mouse

- Show your expression when the lion awakens with a mighty roar.
- Beg the lion not to eat you.
- Say, "Some day I may be able to help you," bravely, yet timidly.
- Nibble one side of the net, then the other, and finally the middle, trying harder and harder to set the lion free.
- Show how your face looks when the lion breaks free.
- Bow to the king, saying, "I was happy to serve you, your majesty."
- Show how your face looks when the lion bows to you.
- Make a frozen picture with the lion and the mouse walking side by side as friends.

Costume Suggestions

Lion: Yellow nylon net material (about two yards) tied around the head for a mane, or strips of yellow or gold felt attached to a hat. Rope for a tail, with end unraveled for the tuft of the tail.

Mouse: Headband with felt or construction-paper mouse ears. Yarn or thin strip of brown cloth for a tail.

Hunters: Safari-style hats or baseball caps of green, brown, or other hunter colors.

Lake: Blue or aqua material held and shimmered by two students.

Palm tree: Green, long-sleeved shirt or green fabric draped and tied around shoulders.

Berry bush: Red, blue, or purple gloves.

Critical-Thinking Questions

1. Who is your favorite character? Why?
2. This is one of the most famous of all of Aesop's fables. Why do you think it is in so many books?
3. What do you think of the lion's behavior toward the mouse in the beginning when she awakens him? Does the lion have good reason to be that angry? Explain.
4. When the mouse says, "Some day I may be able to help you," do you think she really feels she might be able to help the lion someday? Explain.
5. What else might the mouse have said to make the lion let her go?
6. What other things can mice do that lions can't do besides nibbling nets?
7. Were you glad that the lion scared the hunters away? Explain.
8. What part of the fable do you think is the most exciting or dramatic?
9. The lion discovers that "Small things can be the most valuable." What other things in the world are very small and cost no money but make our lives more enjoyable and wonderful because they exist?
10. Why do you think people have called the lion the King of the Jungle for thousands of years? Why isn't some other powerful animal, such as a bear or rhinoceros, King of the Jungle?

Research

These research projects will increase students' understanding of the characters.

• Find other fables or stories in which the lion is treated as King and the other animals obey him.
• Find a story in which the lion is a good or just king. What does that lion do that shows he is wise, fair, or good?
• Find a story in which the lion is a bad, prideful, domineering king. What does he do that angers others?
• Mice are characters in books perhaps more than any other animals. Why do you think so? Find another mouse story that you like and share it with the class. How does the author treat the mouse character? Is the mouse helpful, clever, mischievous or evil?

Creating Art

Paper Plate Mask of the Lion
Materials: Paper plate, fast-drying glue, paint or crayons, materials for decoration such as different kinds of pasta, dried beans, colored candies, shells, beads, buttons, yarn, ribbon, fabric,

and colored paper; tape and string if the mask is to be worn.

Goal: To make an African mask that captures the character of the lion.

Method: Show students a book of African masks. A good one is *African Masks* by Robert Bleakley. Point out that these masks don't look exactly like the animal, but capture its feeling or spirit. Ask students to note the different patterns on the masks and how these patterns make the eyes stand out. Ask, "Why do you think the artist makes the eyes stand out?"

Tell students to think about different patterns and materials they might like to use and to think about enhancing the eyes. Have students bring in materials from home. They can make a sketch of their masks, planning where to put different decorations.

Have students determine where the eye holes should be on their masks and cut them out. Then let them paint or color the plates the desired color. They should paint the eyes first to make them stand out, then add the decorations. If desired, students may cut out and add ears, using part of another plate.

If students want to wear their masks or display them as art objects, show them how to attach an elastic band or a string. If students wear their masks while acting, the movements of their bodies must be very exaggerated to show the characters' actions and feelings. Students may want to look at pictures of people from early cultures dancing with animal masks. Display all the masks on the chalkboard tray. Discuss how they capture the feeling of the lion. What colors, patterns, or materials were used that made them effective?

Drama Follow-up in Pairs
(all grades)

Cast of Characters:

The lion in the fable
Bob Lion, his friend

Tell students, "One of you will be the lion in the fable. Let's call him Leo. The other will be his friend Bob Lion. Bob just saw Leo walking with a mouse. Bob doesn't think it is lionly behavior for a royal lion to stroll along with a mere mouse. Think about what the characters will do and say in this new story. Act out this new story, including this beginning, middle, and end:

"Beginning: Bob Lion pads over to Leo's den and says he wants to talk to him. Leo agrees.

"Middle: Bob explains that it's unlionly for Leo to walk with a mouse, and tells him why. Leo explains why he's doing so.

"End: Bob and Leo come to a new understanding of the situation, and they part as friends."

Can you become the lion overpowering the mouse?
Can you become the mouse with the lion overpowering you?
What could you say?

Dramatizing Aesop's Fables

Can you claw the net like the lion trying to get free?
What sounds and motions would show this?

Dramatizing Aesop's Fables

The Hare and the Tortoise

by Aesop

adapted by Louise Thistle

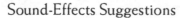

Cast of Characters (four or more):

Narrators (one or more)

Hare

Tortoise

Badger

Other forest animals (as many as desired)

Optional objects: Tortoise's hole, Hare's house,

tree Hare sleeps under, finish line

(Two students might play all the objects and minor characters.)

Sound-Effects Suggestions

Vocal sounds or sounds made with objects: Tap a glass with a spoon for Hare leaping;
pound a desk gently with fist for Tortoise plodding.

Rhythm instruments: Use a triangle for Hare leaping, wood block and mallet for
Tortoise plodding.

Staging Suggestion: If you are using the Dramatizing Stories as Plays method with
individuals cast in each role, you might begin the race at the front of the room
and go around the room's edge, with Hare sleeping two-thirds of the way around.

A *pesky* hare was always jumping up and down, saying, "I'm so fast.
No one can beat me." Every day he would point a paw at Tortoise and
sing, "Slow poke, slow poke. Tortoise is a slow poke."

Tortoise would stick his head out and frown. This made Hare sing
louder, "Tortoise is a slow poke."

The animals were sick of that hare. "What a *pest*," they would say.

One day Badger waddled to Tortoise's house and whispered something. Tortoise nodded, liking Badger's idea.

The next morning Tortoise crawled to Hare's house and called,
"Get up!" Hare grumbled, because he liked to sleep late. But seeing

Dramatizing Aesop's Fables

Tortoise, he yelled, "Tortoise is a slow poke." This time Tortoise said politely, "I am probably the slowest thing alive. But let's race to prove it."

Hare thought he would fall apart laughing. His stomach laughed, "Ha, ha, ha, ha." His head laughed, "Ha, ha, ha, ha." His tail laughed, "Ha, ha, ha, ha." He looked at his tail. He thought it had popped off from laughing so hard.

Hare hopped to the starting line. "Let's go," he yelled. Slowly, Tortoise crawled up. "Slow poke," said Hare. But Tortoise just stuck his head out.

Badger called, "One, two, three, go!" and they were off. In two leaps, Hare was halfway around the track. In three, he was almost to the finish.

Now the lazy hare yawned. He saw a big tree. Hare stretched out and fell alseep.

Tortoise kept plodding along. With every step he sang, "I won't give up. I won't give up. I won't give up."

When he reached Hare, Tortoise put a claw to his mouth, "Shhhh," so no one would wake him. Then he tip-clawed past him.

Soon he came to the finish line. He started to put a claw over when suddenly Hare awoke. "Oh, no!" he screeched, and made one leap to win. But too late! Tortoise put his claw over the finish line first.

The animals cheered.

Badger put a blue ribbon around Tortoise's neck. Hare's head went down, down, down. Tortoise never bragged about winning. But he always wore his blue ribbon just to remind Hare who the winner was. 🐌

Dramatizing the Story

Becoming the Characters

Show students a picture of each character and discuss its attributes. Refer to the information provided. Then give students the following directions to let them become each character.

Hare Information: Hares have long hind legs, long ears that turn to hear everything, twitching noses and big eyes always checking for enemies. Sometimes they hop all over and seem scatterbrained. Silly people are sometimes called hare-brained.

Becoming Hares

- Show with your ears, eyes, and nose what a rabbit would do when looking for enemies.
- Pull up a carrot with your front paws.
- Munch it with your blunt front teeth. Twitch your nose to make sure no one is near.
- Take two hops back to your rabbit hole. Freeze, holding perfectly still so that no one will see you.

Tortoise Information: Tortoises are even slower than turtles, taking five hours to go one mile. They can live 100 years, because their hearts beat slowly and their bodies move slowly. Tortoises have round, strong legs. They pull their heads into their shells to protect themselves. They live in underground burrows. They eat plants — even cactus — to get water.

Becoming Tortoises

- Tuck your head and claws into your shell.
- Slowly push them out, looking around for enemies all the time.
- In place, crawl on your sturdy legs — one foot after the other, one foot after the other, one foot after the other. Freeze.
- Stretch out your long neck, looking for food. Look left and right.
- See a cactus. Take a bite and chew the tough plant slowly. Take another bite and chew.
- Oops, you see a coyote; pull your head and claws back into your shell and freeze.

Becoming Forest Animals

Decide what kind of forest animal you are. How does the animal move? Does it scurry, trot, crawl, fly, lumber, or make some other movement?

- On a count of three, freeze and show your animal's stance and size.

- On another count of three, make your animal's cheering sound. For example, mice might squeak; owls, whoo; blue-jays, squawk; squirrels, chatter; bears, roar. Freeze — open your mouth without a sound to look like your animal cheering.

Reenacting Moments from the Story

Hare's Moments

- Put your paws on your hips and say, "I'm so fast. I'm so fast."
- Point a paw and sing, "Slow poke. Slow poke. Tortoise is a slow poke."
- Laugh like a boastful hare — laugh with your stomach, "Ha, ha, ha." Laugh with your head. Laugh with your tail. Check to see if your tail has popped off. Freeze as you look.
- Take one big leap in place with your hind legs. Take a second leap and freeze in the middle of the leap to make a picture of Hare in flight.
- Yawn, stretch, and say, "I think I'll take a nap."
- Wake up and see Tortoise about to cross the line. What do you say?
- Take one huge leap in place to beat Tortoise. Show your face when you don't make it.
- Hide in your hole after you lose.
- Show your face when you see Tortoise wearing the blue ribbon.

Tortoise's Moments

- Show your face when Hare calls you a slow poke.

- Show your face when Badger whispers how to beat Hare.
- Ask Hare to have a race. What do you say?
- Plod in place singing, "I won't give up. I won't give up."
- Show your face and what you do when you pass by sleeping Hare.
- Make a frozen picture just as you are about to step over the finish line.
- Show what you do with your body to show victory.
- Show how you look wearing the blue ribbon when Hare passes by.

Badger's Moments

- Waddle to Tortoise and whisper your plan.
- Raise your furry paw and say, "One, two, three, go!" to start the race.
- Show your face and body as you cheer Tortoise on.
- Present tortoise with his ribbon. What do you say?

Costume Suggestions

Hare: Headband with tall paper ears or commercial rabbit ears

Tortoise: Green baseball cap with bill turned backwards

Badger: Brown, gray, or black knit or furry cap

Other animals: Headbands with ears of various colors or different baseball caps of appropriate colors

Critical-Thinking Questions

1. Why do you think Hare boasts? How do you think he became so boastful?
2. Why does Hare make fun of Tortoise and not the other animals?
3. How do you feel about boastful people? Explain.
4. This fable teaches persistence, or not giving up on a difficult task. Describe someone you have known, heard, or read about who worked and worked at a task and finally did it well.
5. One reader is glad the hare lost the race. Another feels sorry for the hare. How do you feel? Explain.
6. Some people have said that the moral of this fable is "slow and steady wins the race." What does that mean?
7. What other ways might the animals have used to teach Hare not to brag and be such a pest?
8. Why do you think Badger knew Tortoise would beat Hare?
9. What do you think is the funniest part of the story? Explain.
10. What part of the story did you find the most exciting or dramatic?
11. This is one of Aesop's most famous fables. Why do you think people tell it so often?
12. Why can't Hare look Tortoise in the eye after Tortoise beats him?
13. Why do you think Tortoise doesn't brag to Hare about beating him?
14. Find out which other fable in this book has a contest. Why do people have contests rather than just bragging or fighting?

Research

• The rabbit is an important character in many Native American stories. Find a Native American story about a rabbit and share it with the class. Is the rabbit in your story silly, clever, a pest? Explain.
• Brer Rabbit is another famous rabbit character. Find a Brer Rabbit story and share it with the class. Find out about the author, Joel Chandler Harris (Uncle Remus), whose life had many similarities to Aesop's, and share this information with the class.
• Walt Disney made a cartoon version of "The Hare and The Tortoise." Watch this cartoon and compare it with the version you have dramatized.

Creating Art

*Shoe-Box Diorama of
"The Hare and Tortoise"*

Materials:

Shoe box
Construction paper
Glue
Modeling clay
Materials such as felt, fabric, cotton balls, stones, and twigs

Goal: To design a "picture frame" stage setting of the story.

Method: Have students take the cover off a shoe box and turn the box on its side. The opening is the "picture frame." Inside is the stage. Have students make a sky or other backdrop for the back of the box — perhaps using fabric or construction paper for the sky and scenery, and cotton balls for clouds. Let students suggest any other materials that could be used to make the backdrop three dimensional.

Let students add a forest floor, perhaps felt or another fabric. Students can put in twigs and little stones, holding them in place with blobs of modeling clay. Ask, "Is there any way to tape a finishing line inside your box?"

Have students draw stand-up figures of the characters, leaving little folds or flaps on the bottom of each one, so that they can stand up on the stage floor. Show students how to fold the flaps and paste the figures in different positions on the set (perhaps one forward and one back) to create dramatic interest. Ask, "What else could you add to your set design?"

Drama Follow-up in Pairs
(for all grades)

Cast of Characters:
Hare
Mr. Owl

Tell students, "Hare is upset because he lost the race to Tortoise. He doesn't want to see Tortoise or the other animals because he is so ashamed. Hare goes to Mr. Owl, a kind teacher, for help. Act out this new story, including this beginning, middle and end:

"Beginning: Hare hops to Mr. Owl's room and tells him why he is ashamed and why he feels no one likes him.

"Middle: Mr. Owl and Hare discuss some ways he might be able to change his behavior and make friends with the other animals.

"End: Hare thanks Mr. Owl for his help. He leaves, remembering two pieces of good advice that will help him get along better with others."

Ask for volunteers to share Mr. Owl's advice to Hare.

(for grades four and above)

Cast of Characters:
Badger
Hare

Tell students, "Badger is going to have a victory dinner for Tortoise and invite a camera crew from the TV station. He needs to have Hare attend because he is the other contestant. Make up a scene in which Badger tries to convince Hare to attend the victory dinner, but Hare is ashamed and tries to get out of it. Include the following beginning, middle, and end in your story.

"Beginning: Badger waddles to Hare's house. Hare is sleeping and doesn't want to see Badger, but finally lets him in.

"Middle: Badger tries to convince Hare to come to the victory dinner for Tortoise. Hare tries to get out of it, giving reasons for not going.

"End: Badger and Hare come to a solution to the problem so that both are satisfied, and Badger leaves."

Ask volunteers to share their solutions.

Can you become the tortoise in this picture?
What might the tortoise say as he passes the hare?
Can you become the hare?
What do you think he is dreaming about?

Dramatizing Aesop's Fables

Can you show how the tortoise feels in this picture?
What might he say?
Can you make a frozen picture of the hare's actions here?
What could he be saying?

The Crow and the Pitcher
by Aesop
adapted by Louise Thistle

Cast of Characters (three or more):
Narrators (one or more)
Crow
Pitcher (one or more)
Water in the pitcher (optional)
Sun (One person might play both
the pitcher and the sun.)

Sound-Effects Suggestions:
Vocal sounds or sounds made with objects: Tap a glass with a spoon for pebbles pinging
against the pitcher; thump a desk for kicking the pitcher; tap a desk or table with
a pencil for pebbles plopping into the water.

Rhythm instruments: Use a triangle for pebbles pinging against the pitcher, a drum
for kicking the pitcher, and a mallet and wood block for pebbles plopping into
water.

A *beautiful* black crow was flying in the hot sun. The sun was burning its rays onto his body. The crow landed and fanned himself with a
wing. Then he hopped along looking for water. "Where's the water?
Where's the water?" he cawed.

Suddenly the crow saw a tall pitcher and looked inside. He saw
water at the bottom. He stuck his beak into the pitcher, but he could
not reach the water. He kept poking and poking his head deeper
down, but he couldn't quite reach it.

The crow walked back and forth, thinking what to do. Then he
thought, "Maybe I can knock the pitcher over. The water will spill out,
and I can get it."

He pushed the pitcher with one wing. Uh! He pushed the pitcher

Dramatizing Aesop's Fables

with the other wing. Uh! He pushed and pushed the pitcher with his whole body. Uhhhhhhhh! But he could not get the pitcher to fall over so that he could get the water out.

The crow was upset and began to caw loudly. Then he saw some pebbles. He thought, "I can break the pitcher with a pebble and get the water out."

He tossed one pebble at the pitcher. Ping! He tossed another pebble. Ping! He tossed a third pebble. Ping! The pitcher seemed to say, "Ouch." But it would not break, and so the water would not spill out.

Now the crow was *very* upset, and he began to cry, "Caw, caw, caw." He knew that this was silly, but he got angry, too. He flew into a rage and flew this way and that all over the place.

Then he kicked the pitcher with one claw, "Ow." He kicked the pitcher with his other claw, "Ow." He banged his head against the pitcher, "Owwwwwwww." Now he was aching all over. "Ow, Ow, Ow." He started to cry.

Suddenly he sat down to cool off. He looked at the pebbles once more.

Then, aha, he stuck a wingtip into the air. He had a great idea. He hopped to the pitcher once more. He put one pebble into the pitcher. Plop. He put a second pebble into the pitcher. Plop. He put a third pebble into the pitcher. Plop. He put a fourth, fifth, and sixth pebble into the pitcher. Plop, plop, plop.

The crow stuck his head into the pitcher. Then he hopped up and down with joy.

Just as he thought, the pebbles on the bottom had made the water in the pitcher rise. The crow put in two more pebbles. Plop, plop. Now the water was up to the top. He stuck his beak in and lapped up every bit of the good, cool water.

Then crow threw back his head and cawed with pleasure. He had used his head and hadn't given up. The triumphant crow flew off into the sunset. He was a smart crow indeed, and he had never felt more refreshed in his life. ✌

Dramatizing the Story

Becoming the Characters

Show students a picture of each character and discuss its attributes. Refer to the information provided. Then give students the following directions to let them become each character.

Crow Information: Crows have black, shiny wings and a strong bill. They are perky, with bold, raucous voices. They are clever. They can imitate people's and animals' sounds, and are known to be able to make twenty-three different kind of sounds.

Becoming the Crow

- Flap and show how proud you are of your beautiful, black, glossy wings.
- Caw three times proudly.
- Say, "Where's the water?" in your raucous voice.

Becoming the Pitcher

- Make your body look like a tall pitcher with a handle and a spout.
- Make a pitcher with two or three people — one or two for the pitcher and another for the water in the bottom. How can you make it look as though the water is rising slowly when the crow puts the pebbles in?

Becoming the Sun

- Make your face, body, and arms look as if you're a hot sun, burning its rays onto the crow.
- Make yourself a quiet setting sun, perhaps turning your back to the audience and sinking slowly.

Re-enacting Moments from the Story

The Crow's Moments

- Show with your face and body how hot you feel flying next to the sun.
- Show how glad you are to find the water.
- Dip your beak deeper down to get the water.
- Show your feeling when you can't get it.
- Think, trying to figure out how to get the water.
- Push the pitcher, first with one wing, then the other wing, and finally with both wings and your whole body. Show greater effort each time.
- In slow motion, kick the pitcher with one claw, then the other, and finally bang your head against it. Freeze, showing your feeling.
- Plop four pebbles into the pitcher.
- Show your excitement as the water

rises to the top. What do you say?
- Drink the water as if you are dying of thirst.
- Make a frozen picture showing how proud you feel flying into the sunset.

Costume Suggestions

Crow: Top of black pantyhose cut off to create a cap, or a black baseball cap
Pitcher: All-white clothes or clothes of a light color
Water: Blue cloth that is moved up as water rises to top
Sun: Yellow, gold, or orange shirt; yellow or orange nylon net; or other material draped and tied around shoulders

Critical-Thinking Questions

1. Why do you think the crow continued to try to get water out of the pitcher when it was so much trouble? Why didn't he look around some other place?
2. One reader said she thought it was strange that the crow couldn't break the pitcher with pebbles. What do you think? Explain.
3. Why did the crow fly into a rage? Why didn't flying into a rage help? Why do people sometimes fly into a rage when they know that it is silly?
4. How do you think the crow thought of putting pebbles into the pitcher?
5. One reader says the crow used his creativity. What does that mean?
6. How else could the crow have gotten water out of the pitcher?

7. What does the expression, "He has something to crow about," mean? How might it apply to the crow at the end of this fable?
8. Have you ever tried to do something that you wanted to do very much that was very difficult? Share your story with someone. Did you continue to try to do it? Why or why not?

Research

- Find a person in a story or in the news who had to work and work to achieve her or his goal. What was the goal? Why do you think that person kept working so hard trying to do it? Describe how you think that person felt after achieving the goal.
- The crow is an important character in Native American stories. Find a Native American story about a crow and share it with the class. What kind of a character is the crow in the Native American story? How is that crow similar to the crow in "The Crow and the Pitcher?" How is it different?

Creating Art

Making Stick Puppets

Materials: Light-weight paper or oaktag, scissors, crayons, tape, and a tongue depressor or ice cream stick.

Goal: To create simple puppets and to act the story using puppets.

Method: Let each student draw the crow, the pitcher, and the sun on tagboard or lightweight paper and cut them out. Explain that the characters should be large enough so that they will be visible to the audience and easy to cut. Tell students to color the crow on both sides so that he can turn and move in both directions. Students can tape the figures to an ice cream stick or tongue depressor.

To perform, students could hide behind a desk or bookcase. One student could narrate the story as another performs, or someone could make up dialogue for the crow. If a student is performing alone, he or she holds the sun in one hand and the crow in another in the beginning. Then the student puts down the sun and picks up the pitcher when the crow sees the pitcher. The pitcher is held in one hand and the crow in the other until the end. When the crow flies off into the sunset, the student puts down the pitcher and picks up the sun again.

Drama Follow-up in Pairs

(for all grades)

Cast of Characters:
Crow
Crow's mother

Tell students, "The crow flies home. He tells his mother about his adventure with the pitcher. She is so proud of him that she gives him his favorite dinner. Act out this new story, including the following beginning, middle and end.

"Beginning: The crow soars home. His mother asks where he has been.

"Middle: The crow tells his mother about his adventure with the pitcher and everything that happened.

"End: The mother is so proud of her boy that she serves him his favorite dinner, and they hop over and eat it."

(for grades four and above)

Cast of Characters:
Mr. Crow
Student

Tell students, "When the crow grows up, he becomes a school counselor because he likes to see people succeed. A teacher sends Mr. Crow a student who is smart but who won't do his work. Mr. Crow is concerned and must convince the student to do the work. Think of what the characters might say and do, and act out this new story, including the following beginning, middle and end.

"Beginning: Mr. Crow is sitting in his office and the discouraged student enters. They greet each other and sit down to talk.

"Middle: Mr. Crow questions the student and the student explains why she or he isn't doing the school work. Mr. Crow gives suggestions, and the two come up with a plan of action that satisfies both.

"End: The student leaves Mr. Crow's office with a new attitude and plan of action."

Ask for volunteers to share their plan of action with the class.

Can you show the crow's expression when he first sees the water?
What could he be saying?

Can you become the crow in this picture and show how he feels?

The Dog and His Reflection

by Aesop
adapted by Louise Thistle

Cast of Characters (four or more):
Narrators (one or more)
Greedy dog
Butcher
Customer
Big dog
Little dog
Greedy dog's reflection
Greedy dog's master
(Two students may play the butcher, the customer,
the big dog and the little dog, and the greedy dog's reflection)

Sound-Effects Suggestions:
Vocal sounds or sounds made with objects: Tap a desk with a pen or a pencil for the dog trotting; hit a glass with a spoon for the steak dropping down.

Rhythm instruments: Use a wood block and mallet for the dog trotting; a triangle to highlight the steak dropping down.

Staging Suggestion: If you are using the Dramatizing Fables as Plays method, you might use one side of the stage area for the butcher shop, the middle for the bridge, and the other side for the doghouse, so that each location is obvious.

O*nce* a greedy dog was trotting by a butcher's shop. He looked in the window and saw a big steak on the counter. His eyes grew big. His tongue hung out. He wanted that steak. The butcher was waiting on a customer. The customer pointed to the steak. The butcher turned to get paper to wrap it.

Then the greedy dog slunk into the shop. He seized the steak in his teeth and trotted out the door. The butcher and customer ran out yelling, "Stop, Stop!" But the greedy dog did not stop. He wagged his tail back and forth to show how proud he was to have the steak.

Other dogs trotted down the street. There was a big dog who barked, "Woof, woof, woof!" There was a little dog who barked, "Yip, yip, yip." They wanted steak, too.

But the greedy dog growled at them, and they ran away. The other dogs were angry and called, "Why are you so greedy? Why are you so greedy? Why are you so greedy?"

But the greedy dog did not care. He stuck his nose up in the air, wagged his tail, and trotted on. Then the greedy dog came to a bridge over a river. He planned to eat his steak the minute he got over the bridge.

But in the middle of the bridge, the greedy dog looked down into the water. There he saw what looked like *another* dog also holding a large steak in his mouth. He cocked his head. He frowned and growled. Little did the greedy dog know that the other dog was himself, and he was looking at his own reflection.

Instead, the greedy dog thought it was another dog with a steak just as big as his. The greedy dog was jealous. He wanted both pieces. He barked to make the other dog drop his steak.

As soon as the greedy dog opened his mouth, his own steak dropped into the water. The greedy dog watched it go down, down, down. He couldn't believe his eyes. His steak had disappeared to the bottom of the river. He threw back his head and howled.

Greedy dog walked across the bridge with his head down low. His master had seen him on the bridge and asked where he had gotten the steak he had dropped. The greedy dog tried to pretend he didn't know what the master was talking about, but the master was too smart to fall for that.

"Bad dog," the master said, and led him to the doghouse. There the greedy dog slept all night with no supper. "I'll never be greedy again. I'll never be greedy again," he whimpered in his sleep all night long. 🐾

Dramatizing Aesop's Fables

Dramatizing the Story

Becoming the Character

Show students a picture of each character and discuss its attributes. Refer to the information provided. Then give students the following directions to let them become each character.

Dog Information: Dogs are bouncy and sometimes trot along with their pink tongues showing. They have lots of pep and often show with their faces, bodies, and voices exactly how they feel.

Becoming the Greedy Dog

- Trot in place like a happy, bouncy dog.
- Stick your tongue out and pant because you are hot and thirsty. Lap cool water from your dog bowl.
- Scratch a flea on your shoulder. Chew some hard dog food.
- Sigh like a tired dog, shake yourself, and curl up in your dog bed and go to sleep.

Becoming a Dog on the Street

- Decide what kind of dog you are. Will you be a poodle, a German shepherd, a cocker spaniel, or some other kind of dog? What color is your coat? Do you have big teeth or little sharp ones? Show them.
- On the count of three, woof and trot in place as the kind of dog you are.
- On another count of three, freeze to show how angry you are at the greedy dog. Make a voiceless growl. Be ready to tell what kind of dog you are — your color, your name, and what you like to eat.

Becoming the Bridge

- Alone or with a partner, become a small bridge that the dog can cross. Are you a straight or a curved bridge? Are you wood, stone, or concrete?

Becoming the Dog's Reflection

In pairs, one student can be the dog and the other can be the reflection. The greedy dog does the following actions slowly, and the other dog tries to follow the first one exactly:

- Look in the water.
- See the other dog with a steak and frown.
- Show your teeth.
- Woof loudly to get the other dog to drop the steak.
- Watch the steak go down, down, down.
- Whimper.

Re-enacting Moments from the Story

The Greedy Dog's Moments

- Show with your eyes how excited you are to see the steak in the shop.
- In place, slink into the butcher's shop quietly.
- Seize the steak in your teeth and trot out the door.
- Show how proud you are to have gotten the steak. Wag your tail.
- Growl in your throat to make the other dogs go away.
- Show your expression as you think you see another dog with a big steak.
- Bark and open your mouth to make the other dog drop his steak.
- Watch your steak drop down, down, down with your head going lower each time.
- Show how you feel when you realize that the steak is gone.
- Show your expression as you try to fool your master about stealing the steak.
- Sit in your doghouse and whimper, "I'll never be greedy again." Show how miserable you feel.

The Butcher's and the Customer's Moments

- Cut and wrap meat for the customer.
- Show your expression when you see that the dog has stolen the meat.
- Say, "Stop, Stop!" to make the dog drop the steak.

The Master's Moments

- Watch the greedy dog drop the steak into the water.
- Say, "Bad dog!" to the greedy dog.
- Take the greedy dog by the collar and lead him to the doghouse.

Costume Suggestions

Greedy dog: Felt, furry material, or paper ears attached to a headband

Dog's reflection: Same costume as the greedy dog's

Butcher: White cook's hat or white sailor hat and cook's apron

Customer: Derby for a man, a flowered hat for a woman

Other dogs: Ears of different sizes and colors attached to an oaktag headband.

Bridge: All brown, black, or gray clothing

Critical-Thinking Questions

1. Why do you think the butcher and customer were surprised that the dog stole the steak?
2. When do you think the greedy dog felt happiest in the story? Explain.
3. When do you think he felt the worst? Explain.
4. Do you think the greedy dog will change his behavior after having spent the night in the doghouse? Explain.
5. Do people expect dogs to be as trustworthy as people? Why or why not?

6. What might have happened to an adult caught stealing a steak, or a child stealing candy?

7. What might the dog's owner do to prevent the dog from stealing again?

8. One reader said she thought it was the owner's fault that the dog stole. What is your opinion? Explain.

9. One reader said he thought this was a sad story. Another found it funny. What do you think? Explain.

10. Have you ever felt greedy for some food or something else and had a bad experience because of it? Share your experience with someone.

11. What makes people greedy? How do people learn not to be so greedy?

Research

• The greedy dog was selfish. Often, however, in stories and in life, dogs are also trustworthy, loyal, and unselfish. Tell about a real dog you know or have heard about or a dog in a story who was helpful and maybe even a hero. What did the dog do? How was the dog rewarded?

• Find another fable or story in which a greedy person or animal gets in trouble. What happens as a result of the animal or person's being greedy?

Creating Art

Meat Tray Picture to Hang
Materials:
Foam meat tray
Construction paper of different colors
Yarn or string
White glue
Scissors
Tape
Wallpaper, felt, or other fabrics, buttons, and beads (optional)

Goal: To imagine and design a picture that would appeal to the dog in the story.

Method: Explain to students that they are going to create a picture on a meat tray that would brighten up the dog-house of the greedy dog and make him feel better. Discuss what the dog might like to have in his picture. It might also be a picture that students would like to have in their own homes.

Give students construction paper and other materials to create the picture. The edge of the tray serves as the picture frame. When the picture is finished, show students how to attach a piece of yarn or string to the back with tape so it can be hung.

Display the pictures at the front of the room and let each student explain to the class why the dog would like her or his picture in the doghouse.

Drama Follow-up in Groups of Three
(all grades)

Cast of Characters:
Butcher
Customer
Greedy dog

Have students enact the following scene: The butcher and customer react to the greedy dog's theft. Tell students to include the following beginning, middle and end in their story:

Beginning: The customer enters the shop and requests a steak. The butcher points out different types of steaks, the customer chooses one, and the butcher turns around to get paper to wrap it. The greedy dog sneaks in and takes the steak.

Middle: The customer and the butcher try to get the greedy dog to stop, but he trots away.

End: The butcher and the customer return to the shop and decide what to do about the stolen steak.

Can you become this dog and show what he is feeling?

Can you do what this dog just did?
Can you make the noise the dog might be making?

Dramatizing Aesop's Fables

The Wind and the Sun

by Aesop
adapted by Louise Thistle

Cast of Characters (four or more):
Narrators (one or more)
Wind
Sun
Person or group of people (One or two students
or the class as a whole might act as the people.)

Sound-Effects Suggestions:
Vocal sounds or sounds made with objects: Blow through the teeth or crumple paper for
the wind blowing; tap a glass with a spoon for the sun shining.

Rhythm instruments: Use a tambourine and a drum for the wind blowing and a
triangle for the sun shining.

Once the big bully wind came along, and he blew three times:
woosh, woosh, woosh. He saw the gentle sun casting down her rays
three times: shine, shine, shine. The bully didn't like to see the sun
enjoy herself. And so he said in a big bully voice, "I want a fight."

The sun didn't want to fight, and so she stepped aside. She put one
ray to her head to think. And then, "Aha," she said. "How about a
contest?"

The bully, who wasn't too bright, said in a big bully voice, "A
contest. What's a contest?"

The sun said, "See those people down there? Let's see who can
make them take their coats off."

"That's a snap," said the bully. And he blew once. But this made the
people button up their coats.

This made the bully angry. So he puffed himself up bigger and
blew twice. But this made the people turn up their collars and pull
themselves in tight against the cold wind.

Now the wind was so furious that he puffed himself up and blew with every bit of himself. His face blew; his shoulders blew. His whole body stretched out and shook and blew and blew and blew. His eyes looked as if they would pop out, he blew so hard. But this made the people bend over and look up in fright at the fierce wind.

Then the sun held up a ray and said, "Let me try." First she sent down one warm ray: shine. Then she sent down two rays: shine, shine. Finally she opened up all her warmest rays and sent them down on the people: shine, shine, shine.

Then the people unbuttoned their coats. They took them off and flung them over their backs. They looked up and said, "What a beautiful sunny day."

The wind was so angry he blew himself away behind a cloud: brrrrrrrr. But before he left, the sun stepped forward and called after him, "Gentleness and kindness will do a lot more for people than violence and force."

The sun stood still and opened up all of her warmest rays on the people, making a beautiful, sunny day.🙶

Dramatizing Aesop's Fables

Dramatizing the Story

Becoming the Characters

Show students a picture of each character and discuss its attributes. Refer to the information provided. Then give students the following directions to let them become each character.

Wind Information: In the time of the ancient Greeks, fierce wind was considered evil. Even today, hurricanes and other big winds can be very destructive.

Becoming the Wind:
- Wake up slowly and become a gentle breeze, blowing softly.
- Make trees sway slightly.
- Become a gale, using your voice and body to knock down trees and capsize boats. What sound effect could you make with your voice to convey furious wind? Freeze, and make a picture of the wind at its most furious.
- Die down to a gentle breeze again, disappearing into the night.

Sun Information: The sun is often considered kind and helpful. In ancient times, people worshiped the sun because of its light and warmth and ability to help crops grow. There are "sun worshippers" today who feel most happy when the sun is out.

Becoming the Sun:
- Be the sun about to rise in the east. Put your head down and rise on a slow count of five. By "five," your rays are fully extended at high noon. Freeze.
- Afternoon is here. To another count of five, set slowly in the west with your head down.

Becoming a Person or the People
- Feel a cool breeze on your arms and neck. Button up your coat. The wind is getting icier. Put up your collar and pull yourself in tight against the icy wind.
- Lean over, being blown in all directions by the heavy gales. Freeze.
- Feel the warm sun on your neck and shoulders. Unbutton your coat. Look up. The bright sun is in your eyes. Take off your coat, and fling it over your shoulder.
- Look up at the bright sun and say, "What a beautiful sunny day."

Re-enacting Characters' Moments

The Wind's Moments
- Say, "I want to fight," like a big bully.
- Say, "A contest. What's a contest?" like a stupid bully.

- Show your expression when you are defeated.

The Sun's Moments

- Show your expressions as you think of a way to avoid a fight with the bully.
- Cast down one warm ray. (Perhaps reach one arm up and wiggle rays down).
- Now cast two warm rays. (Perhaps use two arms.)
- Finally open up and cast all your warmest rays down. (What kind of gesture might show this?)
- Say, "Shine, shine, shine," to soothe the people below.
- Say, "Gentleness and kindness will do a lot more for people than violence and force," to tell the wind the truth.
- Make a frozen picture as you cast all your rays to help and comfort the people below.

Costume Suggestions

Sun: Yellow or gold netting fabric draped around shoulders

Wind: A piece of dark blue, gray, or black cloth whipped around to show the wind howling

Person: Jacket or sweater (Putting one of these on could be mimed.)

Critical-Thinking Questions

1. One reader says the wind is funny. Another says the wind is scary. What do you think? Explain.
2. What might cause someone to be a bully?
3. The sun used a clever trick to stop the wind from being a bully. What else might the sun have done to keep the wind from using force?
4. Why does the story say the wind wasn't too bright? (What are two different meanings of bright?)
5. Why does gentleness and kindness work better than violence and force? Why don't some people remember this?
6. Why would you say the sun is stronger than the wind in this story? How was the sun able to trick the wind?
7. Share an incident in which a thoughtful person was able to break up a fight or relax a tense situation by remaining calm. What kind of techniques did the person use? Explain the situation.
8. Early cultures considered the sun and the wind gods. Why do you think they did so?

Research

- In earliest times, people fought to prove who was strongest or best. Find out when people first began having athletic contests or competitions to prove who was best. Do you think the Olympics might have something to do with this?
- Native Americans worshiped the sun. Find a Native American story that

shows sun worship. What kinds of actions did the people in the story do to show their reverence for the sun?

- The Aztecs made beautiful gold sun effigies as part of their worship of the sun. Find out why they did this and how they used the effigies. Get pictures or models of these to share with the class.

Creating Art

Ocean Scene of Wind or Sun Using Crayon Resist

Materials:

Watercolor paints
Heavy white paper
Crayons
Pictures of the ocean in different kinds of weather

Goal: To explore the technique of crayon resist and discover how it can help depict a sunny or gloomy ocean scene.

Method: Show students pictures of the ocean in different kinds of weather and discuss how the ocean and the sky look different on a gloomy, foggy, windy day than on a bright sunny day. Ask students to decide whether to create a sunny ocean scene or a mysterious gloomy one and how to capture the mood.

Ask, "For example, what colors could you use for the ocean to depict each scene? How might the waves look different? What objects could you put in your scene to capture the mood or feeling of a windy, choppy day compared to a bright golden one?"

Have students draw their scenes with crayons, leaving the sky blank. They might also leave some uncrayoned spaces in the ocean.

Then suggest that students paint the sky with watery blue or some other gentle color for a sunny day and watery black or gray for a mysterious gloomy one. Have students notice how the paint rolls off the places where the crayon is, and look at the different textures the paint and crayon creates.

Drama Follow-up in Pairs
(grades four and above)

Cast of Characters:
Delegate A
Delegate B
Wind (teacher)

Tell students to enact the following scene: Two delegates to the League of Weathers try to calm Wind down.

Have students include the following beginning, middle, and end in their story:

Beginning: Two smart delegates greet each other and discuss the problem of Wind's horrible habit of destroying things with big blustery blowing.

Middle: The two delegates draw up two lists. The first list includes three good reasons why Wind must stop blowing so hard. The second list gives three reasons why gentle or medium winds can be helpful.

End: The two delegates present their lists to Wind to try to convince Wind to stop blowing so hard.

Can you become one of these people and show
feeling the icy wind blowing through your cloak?
Can you make a frozen picture showing
being blown all about in the wind?

Dramatizing Aesop's Fables

Can you make believe the hot sun is blazing down
into your eyes and making your body damp?
Can you make a frozen picture showing how you feel?

The Fox and the Stork

by Aesop
adapted by Louise Thistle

Cast of Characters (four or more):
Narrators (one or more)
Fox
Stork
Plate (one or two)
Vase (one or two; the same actor might play
 both plate and vase)
Doors to the fox's and stork's homes (optional)

Sound-Effects Suggestions:
Vocal sounds or sounds made with objects: Use voice for the phone ringing; tap a glass
with a spoon for the clock chiming; knock on a desk for door knocking.

Rhythm instruments: Use bells for the phone ringing, a triangle for the clock chiming,
and a mallet and wood block for door knocking.

Staging Suggestion:
Use one half of the stage area for Fox's house, and the other for Stork's, so that
there are two distinct house areas.

O*ne* day a fox telephoned the stork next door. The fox laughed
under his breath, "Heh, heh, heh," and invited the stork to dinner. The
stork thanked the fox and was eager to go.

The stork spent the whole day grooming her feathers and looking
in the mirror. She wanted to look her best for the meal.

At six o'clock, the stork fluffed her tail, flew to the fox's house, and
knocked on the door with a wing tip. The fox opened the door. Then
with a sweeping gesture, he led the stork to the dining room.

The stork sniffed delicious beef soup. Her eyes got big, and her
beak opened and closed as she thought about the meal.

Dramatizing Aesop's Fables

But when she walked into the dining room to sit down, she saw only one wide plate on the table. The stork knew that it was too flat for her to get her long beak into. She frowned at the fox.

But the fox just curled his body around the plate and greedily lapped up all the soup. Then he smiled and said, "I'm sorry you didn't eat more."

The stork was annoyed, but didn't say anything. Instead she cocked her head and invited the fox to her house for dinner the next night. The fox bowed. He loved a free meal.

The next night, promptly at six o'clock, the fox straightened his whiskers and trotted to the stork's house. He licked his lips, thinking of a big meal.

The stork opened the door and made a sweeping gesture with a wing tip to the dining room. The fox smelled fish soup. His eyes grew big, and he panted.

But when he sat down, his eyes opened wide with horror. The soup was in a tall vase with a long, long neck. The fox knew that he couldn't get his snout into that deep vase. He growled under his breath, but he didn't dare say anything.

The stork dipped her long beak into the vase, tipped her head back and let the soup run slowly down her throat. Every once in a while, she said, "Yum, yum, yum," in her high voice. The fox was now so hungry that his long tongue hung out, and he drooled.

Then the stork dabbed her beak with a napkin and led the fox to the door.

The stork said, "I hope you enjoyed the meal." The fox grumbled, "Oh, yes, yes, yes." Then he went home with his head down and his tail between his legs. He had never felt hungrier in his life. He decided not to play practical jokes on storks anymore. 🐾

Dramatizing the Story

Becoming the Characters

Show students a picture of each character and discuss its attributes. Refer to the information provided. Then give students the following directions to let them become each character.

Fox Information: Red foxes have fur that is almost a flame-red color. They have white chests, bushy tails, and erect ears. They are smart and crafty. Foxes trot on their toes. They can also gallop on their long, thin legs for short distances at thirty miles an hour.

Becoming Foxes

- Show with your eyes, nose, and body that you are a tricky fox.
- In place, trot lightly and hungrily, looking around for food.
- See a chicken, crouch, and pounce on it. Holding the chicken in your mouth, trot quickly back to your den.
- Toss the chicken into your den, and look out to make sure that no one has followed you.
- Slink inside and close the door quietly.

Stork Information: Storks are tall, white, graceful birds. They have large wings, long thin legs, long necks, and bills good for digging deep. To drink, they fill their beaks with the liquid and then tip their beaks up and let the liquid run down their throats.

Becoming Storks:

- Flap your huge white wings to take off. Soar over the water with your wings outstretched.
- Look down into the water. See a fish. Swoop down and seize it. Oops, it wiggled away. Land. Dig deep down into the mud of the river bank with your bill to get little animals and plants. Tip your beak up and let the food run down into your throat.
- Clean and smooth your feathers with your long bill.
- Put your head under your wing and fall asleep.

Becoming the Plate and the Vase

- One or two of you become a wide, flat plate.
- Transform yourself into a thin vase with no room for the fox's snout.

Re-enacting Moments from the Story
The Fox's Moments

- Show with your eyes that you're a tricky fox and say, "Heh, heh, heh,"

under your breath as you plan to trick someone.
- Slink along like a fox thinking up a trick. Make a sweeping bow and say "Good evening," like a fox pretending to be sincere.
- Greedily curl your body around the plate so that no one else can have any soup. Lap it up quickly with your long tongue.
- Smile and say in a tricky voice, "I'm sorry you didn't eat more."
- Straighten your whiskers and trot to the stork's house.
- Make your eyes look eager as you smell a delicious fish soup. Pant with excitement.
- Show your expression when you see the vase and realize that you can't get your snout in.
- Say, "Yes, yes, yes," to pretend to the stork that you found nothing wrong with her meal.
- Make a frozen picture with your face and body as you leave the stork's house. What kind of sound do you make under your breath?

The Stork's Moments:
- Show your huge white wings and flap them slowly as you reach to answer the phone and answer it with a wing tip.
- Say, "Thank you," politely and pleasantly.
- Groom your wings, daintily biting the bugs out and smoothing down the feathers. Then fluff your tail feathers to get ready for the fox's meal.

- Open and close your bill as you smell the beef soup.
- Show your expression when you see the wide, flat plate.
- Show your expression as you control your feelings. Then politely invite the fox to dinner.
- Show your expression as you bring the fox into your dining room.
- Fill your bill with soup, then tip up your bill and let the soup run down your throat. Dab your beak with the napkin.
- Say sweetly, "I hope everything was all right with the meal."
- Make a frozen picture showing your face when the fox leaves your home.

Costume Suggestions
Fox: Red or orange baseball cap or visor or a snappy-looking hat of any kind

Stork: White baseball cap or pink visor; white shawl, or white nylon netting draped and tied around shoulders

Objects: All-black pants and top for the vase and the plate

Critical-Thinking Questions
1. Why do you think the fox wanted to trick the stork?
2. Why do you think the stork trusted the fox in the beginning?
3. Do you think the fox's trick was funny? Explain.
4. Why didn't the stork say anything to the fox when the stork tricked her?
5. Would you call the stork mean for playing a trick on the fox? Explain.

6. Why did the stork eat her soup slowly when the fox was watching?

7. Can you think of any other way that the stork could have tricked the fox without physically harming him?

8. One reader says she doesn't think the fox will ever play any more practical jokes. Another says she thinks he will. What do you think? Explain.

9. How can someone avoid being tricked by a trickster? Discuss this problem with a neighbor and share your ideas with the class.

10. Would it be uncomfortable to have someone like the fox as a best friend? Why or why not?

11. Why do you think people consider foxes tricky? Do people think of storks as tricky? Why or why not?

Research

• April Fool's Day is a day devoted to playing practical jokes. When and how did April Fool's Day get started? Why do you think we continue to have a day devoted to playing practical jokes?

• Look up the meaning of the word *practical* in the dictionary. What does it mean?

• Look for other stories with a fox as the main character. Find a story in which a tricky fox succeeds with his sly trick. Find one in which the fox gets caught and punished. See if you can find a story in which the fox is the hero.

Creating Art
Creating the Plate and the Vase from Clay

Materials:

Modeling clay
Pictures of Greek pots and vases

Goal: To create original versions of the plate and the vase in the fable through the medium of clay.

Method: Discuss with the class how the ancient Greeks made beautiful pots and vases that were often used for drinking and holding water, olive oil, and other substances. If possible, show pictures of some of the styles of these wonderfully decorated vases. (Students might give reports on the vases and containers.)

Let students use modeling clay to make the kind of container the fox might have used to served soup. Then have students make the kind of container the stork used to serve soup. Finally, tell them to make the kind of container they would like to use to serve soup. Students might shape the entire plate or vase from one piece of clay by squeezing, rolling, pinching, and pulling off unneeded pieces. Or they might blend several pieces of clay together.

Dramatizing Aesop's Fables

Drama Follow-up In Pairs
(for all grades)

Cast of Characters:

Mr. Squirrel
Ms. Chipmunk

Tell students to enact this scene: Freddie Fox, a student at Animal Elementary, is bothering the teacher and the students in class with his tricks and bad behavior. Mr. Squirrel, the teacher, and Ms. Chipmunk, the principal, are trying to think of ways to help Freddie become a better citizen. Have students include the following beginning, middle, and end in their story.

Beginning: Mr. Squirrel comes to Ms. Chipmunk's office and tells her some of the things Freddie has been doing to annoy the class.

Middle: Mr. Squirrel and Ms. Chipmunk discuss ways to help Freddie to become a better citizen.

End: Mr. Squirrel and Ms. Chipmunk tell the class three ideas for helping Freddie help himself and others.

(for grades four and above)

Cast of Characters:

Ms. Stork
Mr. Fox

Tell students to enact this scene: Mr. Fox has become a used motorcycle salesman. Ms. Stork wants to buy a used motorbike, and visits the showroom of Mr. Fox. Have students include the following beginning, middle, and end in their story:

Beginning: Ms. Stork flies into the motorcycle showroom and is greeted by Mr. Fox, the salesman. She tells him that she wants a good used motorbike and why she needs it. Mr. Fox is eager to serve her.

Middle: Mr. Fox tries to convince Ms. Stork to buy a deluxe $5,000 used motorbike. Ms. Stork loves the bike but feels that Mr. Fox is trying to trick her into paying too much. The two bargain on the price. Mr. Fox and Ms. Stork finally make a deal agreeable to both.

End: They both wave as Ms. Stork drives off on the bike she bought, a satisfied customer.

Can you pose like this fox? What is he saying?
Now pose like the stork. What is she thinking?

Dramatizing Aesop's Fables

Can you pose like the stork? What is she saying?
Can you pose like the fox? What is he mumbling under his breath?

Dramatizing Aesop's Fables

The Ant and the Dove

by Aesop
adapted by Louise Thistle

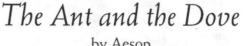

Cast of Characters (four or more):
Narrators (one or more)
Ant
Dove
Bubbling brook
Water reed
Leaf
Bird trapper
(The bubbling brook, the water reed, the leaf, and the
 bird trapper may be played by the same one or two actors.)

Sound-Effects Suggestions:
Vocal sounds or sounds made with objects: Tap a desk with a fingernail for the ant creeping; tap a glass with a spoon for the dove hopping; shake a container with rice for the trapper sneaking through the grass.

Rhythm instruments: Use a mallet and wood block for the ant creeping, a triangle for the dove hopping, and maracas or shakers for the trapper sneaking through the grass.

A_n ant was creeping through the tall grasses. Creep, creep, creep. A brook was bubbling. Bubble, bubble, bubble. The ant was thirsty. She slid down a long water reed to get to the water.

But then, plop! She fell into the water and onto her back. She kicked her six legs high into the air. She cried and cried in her tiny voice for help.

A beautiful dove came flying along. Whirr, whirr, whirr. She stopped and cooed as if to say, "I'll help, I'll help." The dove hopped along looking for a way to help the ant. The ant rocked this way and that in the strong current. She called for help again.

Dramatizing Aesop's Fables

The dove saw a tree with big leaves. She flew up and plucked the biggest leaf and tossed it to the ant. The ant struggled onto the leaf and floated up and down, up and down to shore. The ant bobbed her antennae to thank the dove. The dove fanned the ant with her wings to dry her off. They smiled at each other.

But just then a bird trapper came sneaking through the brush with a bow in one hand. Sneak, sneak, sneak. The trapper got behind the dove. He took an arrow from his quiver and placed it in the bow.

The ant scurried to the trapper's leg and bit him hard. The trapper yelled, "Ouch!" and shot the arrow straight into the air. He ran into the forest, rubbing the painful ant bite.

The dove saw what the ant had done. She thanked and thanked her, flapping her wings and bowing her head.

The ant raised one of her six legs and said, "You saved my life, too. Of course I wanted to help you."

Then the dove flapped a wing good-bye and flew off into the forest. The ant waved one of her six legs good-bye. She knew that they would remain friends forever, because, as she called to her new friend, "A friend in need is a friend indeed." &

Dramatizing Aesop's Fables

Dramatizing the Story

Becoming the Character

Show students a picture of each character and discuss its attributes. Refer to the information provided. Then give students the following directions to let them become each character.

Ant Information: Ants are tiny, with six legs, a big head, and big eyes. They have strong jaws, and can carry things larger than themselves. They are speedy, and use antennae to sense their way around. They are organized; everyone has a special job to do in their ant society.

Becoming Ants

- Hunch over to look like a little ant. Show with your fingers and joints that you have six legs.
- Bob your antennae and pick up a huge bread crumb with your tough jaw. In place, march along behind the other ants in your group to bring the bread back to the colony.

Dove Information: Doves are gentle, graceful, and peaceful. They coo to communicate.

Becoming Doves

- Flap your wings and coo like a gentle dove. Hop lightly along the bank of the brook. Bob your head from side to side, looking for enemies.
- Pluck a branch from an olive tree and soar with it through the air. Look down at the people beneath you and land. Freeze with your head proudly in the air, displaying your olive branch.

Becoming the Trapper

Trapper Information: Trappers are cautious and sneak up quietly to catch their prey.

- Carrying your bow, sneak through the brush without making a sound.
- See the dove and hide. Quickly take an arrow from your quiver and place it in your bow. Freeze.
- Aim carefully and shoot. At the same time, show that you've been bitten hard on your leg by an ant.

Becoming the Brook, the Leaf, and the Water Reed

- Make your fingers, arms and body look like a bubbling brook. Say "Bubble, bubble, bubble," making it sound as though you're bubbling.
- Become the brook bubbling faster when the ant falls in.
- In pairs or alone, become a big leaf. (A student could kneel or stoop so that the ant can pretend to crawl on.)

- Make it look as if you are floating on top of the water.
- Become a tall water reed, bending this way and that lightly and slowly in the breeze.

Re-enacting Moments from the Story

The Ant's Moments

- Show with your face and body that you are very thirsty.
- Show how scared you are when you fall into the brook. Kick your six legs into the air and bob your antennae as if you are drowning.
- Say "Help, Help!" in a scared-to-death, tiny voice. Freeze.
- Say, "Thank you, thank you," to the dove for saving your life.
- Show your strong jaws and how angry you are at the trapper. Bite him hard.
- Say "A friend in need is a friend indeed," to show that you want to remain friends with the dove forever.

The Dove's Moments

- Show with your face and wings how much you want to help the ant. Say, "I'll help you."
- Show how you would look for something with which to help save the ant.
- Fly up to the tree. Pluck off the biggest leaf and toss it to the ant. Watch it float down.
- Express wanting to comfort the ant as you dry her with your wings.

- Say, "Thank you, thank you," to show how grateful you are to the ant for saving your life.
- Show that you want to stay friends with the ant forever as you wave a wing good-bye.

Costume Suggestions

Ant: The top of a pair of black pantyhose can be cut off and worn like a cap on the head. Black gloves can create the feeling of many legs. A headband with bobbing feelers can be used for antennae.

Dove: Use a gray or white baseball hat or pink visor for bill. A beige or gray shawl or gray material may be tied and worn around the shoulders for wings.

Bird Trapper: Use a safari hat or baseball cap.

Water Reed: Wear a green shirt or tie green material around the shoulders or waist.

Brook: Use blue material or strips of blue material or wiggle blue crepe paper for a bubbling effect.

Critical-Thinking Questions

1. In what other Aesop fable in this book does the smallest creature prove to be strong? In what other ways are these two fables similar? How are they different?
2. Why do you think Aesop chose a dove rather than another kind of bird to help the ant in his story?

3. Why do you think the dove wanted to help the ant?

4. What other objects besides a leaf might the dove have used to save the ant?

5. Why was the ant eager to help the dove?

6. Was it the ant's duty to help the dove? Explain.

7. Could an ant really cause so much trouble to a trapper? Explain. What other insect or small creature can cause people trouble? How?

8. What does "A friend in need is a friend indeed" mean? In the dictionary, look up the meaning of "indeed." What did it mean originally?

9. Tell the class or the person sitting next to you how someone helped you when you really needed it.

10. Why do you think some people go out of their way to help out another person?

11. What is the overall mood or tone of this fable? Is it funny, sad, gentle? Explain.

Research

- Find out why the dove has been associated with peace. What is the earliest mention of the dove as a bird of peace?

- Ants are considered industrious. Research and find a fable about hard-working ants and share it with the class. Read a science book about ants and explain to the class how ants spend a day, and what they do that shows that they work hard.

Creating Art

Crayon Leaf Rubbings

Materials:
Lightweight paper
Brightly colored crayons without wrappers
Leaves of various kinds

Goal: To experience the natural wonder of leaves and to use them in a new, creative way.

Method: Bring in as many different kinds of leaves as possible. Show students how to place the leaves under lightweight paper and rub over them with bright crayons. Have students observe the different patterns. Ask, "Which of the leaves do you prefer for doing this activity? Why?" Have students make a design using several leaves.

Variations:

1. Have students create a page or two of rubbings of different leaves and label them by the tree or bush they came from.

2. Have students create a whole tree, using one leaf for the basic design. To do this, students should place a leaf where the leaves would go at the top of a tree and rub, then move the leaf around to different positions at the tree top, rubbing and overlapping as they go. Soon the picture will look like a treetop full of leaves. If desired, a tree trunk could be added at the bottom of the leaf rubbings.

3. Show students how to create insects, animals, and even people with different kinds of leaves by adding a few

details in black crayon. For example, a butterfly can be made by putting a leaf under the paper in two different positions to make wings, then adding the body and antennae with black crayon. Several leaf shapes in a circle make a flower, to which students can add a stem and leaves. A fish can be created using an oval leaf for the basic body shape and the same or another leaf for fins. A leaf with many veins makes good seaweed for the fish to swim through.

4. Have students make a cartoon-person leaf, adding facial and other necessary features.

Save Our Wild Animals Poster

Materials:

Heavy paper

Watercolor paints

Black marking pen

Goal: To realize the beauties and wonders of nature and the importance of saving the earth. (This assignment might be done in conjunction with the first Drama Follow-up).

Method: Ask students to imagine a scene with forest animals that might convince people to save our wildlife. Have students sketch the scene and then finalize their sketches with black marking pens when they look the way they want them. Have students color in their pictures with watercolors and make a poster by giving their pictures a slogan. Ask students to explain why they picked their scenes and slogans to try to convince people to care.

Drama Follow-up in Pairs
(all grades)

Cast of Characters:

Ant

Dove

Tell students to enact the following scene: The ant and the dove decide to try to convince people not to trap or hurt wild animals. Have students include the following beginning, middle, and end in their story:

Beginning: The ant and the dove meet and discuss what happened to them in the fable. The dove tells the ant how she feels after her bad experience with the trapper.

Middle: The ant and the dove decide that they want to convince others not to hurt wild animals.

End: Each animal thinks up one good reason to use to persuade people to be kind or considerate to animals.

Can you make yourself look as concerned as this dove?
What do you think she is saying?
Can you show with only your eyes and hands how the ant feels?

Dramatizing Aesop's Fables

Can you become this young man? What do you think he is saying?
Can you make a frozen picture showing how he feels?

The City Mouse and the Country Mouse

by Aesop
adapted by Louise Thistle

Cast of Characters (four or more):
Narrators (one or more)
Country Mouse
City Mouse
Cat
Trees
Tall buildings (The person who plays the cat might
 also play trees and buildings and make sound effects.)

Sound-Effects Suggestions:
Vocal sounds: Use voice to create birds tweeting, trees whistling, a telephone
ringing, cows mooing, and traffic noises.

Rhythm instruments: Use bells for a telephone ringing and a triangle for the elevator
going up and down, stopping at each floor.

Staging Suggestion: Use one half of the stage for the country mouse's house, and the
other half for the city mouse's house. The mice could drive their car around the
edge of the classroom to show travel back and forth.

One day the country mouse was rocking in her rocker. Birds tweeted.
Cows mooed. Trees swayed and whistled in the wind. It was so pleas-
ant, the mouse telephoned her city cousin to come for a visit.

The city mouse was dancing around his apartment when the telephone rang. He grabbed it and shouted, "What's happening?" The
country mouse invited her cousin to come down for a visit.

"I'm on my way," the city mouse yelped. He whooshed down the
elevator, hopped into his sports car, and zoomed off. His car bumped
up and down the dusty country roads. He was panting for a soda pop.
But when he jumped out at his cousin's, he put a paw up in amaze-
ment. He saw no shops, no restaurants. Was this outer space?

The country mouse ambled out slowly. She greeted her cousin and

Dramatizing Aesop's Fables

pointed out the beautiful trees swaying in the wind.

The country mouse led the city mouse inside to the kitchen table. She proudly served a country meal of vegetable stew, wheat bread, and strawberries. But the city mouse turned up his long nose and said, "Let's try the city for *real* food."

The country mouse hid her hurt feelings and climbed into the car. Her fur almost jumped off, the way the car bumped up and down.

When they got to the city, the city mouse pointed up at the great, tall buildings. The country mouse looked up. They looked like monsters to her. The traffic noises made her ears ache.

The city mouse hurried his cousin into the apartment building and into the elevator. The country mouse held her stomach as the elevator zoomed up.

The city mouse led his cousin inside his apartment to a big table loaded with fancy foods. He pointed to cheeses, biscuits, and big cakes to eat. The country mouse's eyes got big with excitement.

The mice hopped onto the table. They nibbled cheeses. They gnawed biscuits. They lapped up cream. The country mouse ate so much she felt sick. But the city mouse just handed her a dinner mint.

The country mouse was biting into the mint when something touched her back. She turned in horror to see the paw of a big, white cat. "Run!" yelled the city mouse, scurrying into a mouse hole. The country mouse scurried in behind him.

The cat slunk over and stuck a paw into the hole, trying to grab the mice. The country mouse quivered. The cat couldn't quite reach them, meowed, and slunk away.

Soon, the city mouse poked his head out and hopped back onto the table. But the country mouse ran to the door. "Where are you going?" called her cousin. "Home!" said the country mouse. "City life is too fast for me." The city mouse laughed. "Hey, the fun's just starting."

When the country mouse returned home, she sat on her porch and rocked and rocked, happy to be back in her peaceful home. Back in the city, her cousin danced around, looking forward to a lively night on the town. 🐾

Dramatizing the Story

Becoming the Characters

Show students a picture of each character and discuss its attributes. Refer to the information provided. Then give students the following directions to let them become each character.

Country and City Mouse Information: The mice in this story act mouse-like, scurrying into a mouse hole and nibbling foods. They also behave like different kinds of people — one slow-moving and -talking and the other quick-moving and fast-talking.

Becoming the Country Mouse

- Make your body mouse-like. In place, take a few steps very slowly as if you are daydreaming. Freeze.
- Take three big, slow breaths of country air. Feel the warm breeze blowing through your fur.
- Pick up a telephone and dial very slowly. Say, "Howdy," in a slow country-style voice.
- Sit in your rocker and rock, rock, rock in the warm sun. Hum a little tune. Stretch your paws up, yawn, and fall asleep.

Becoming the City Mouse

- Make your body mouse-like. Dance in place to a fast-city beat.
- Grab the telephone and answer it, saying, "Hey, man," to show how cool you are.
- Look in the mirror and spruce up your fur and whiskers. Put on a cool hat and check out how it looks in the mirror.
- Dance to the door and open it, ready for action. Freeze.

Cat Information: Cats slink along quietly, trying to make themselves invisible so that their prey can't see them. They hide and crouch low, and when their prey is unaware, they spring and pounce on it.

Becoming the Cat

- Be a big, sneaky cat crouching behind a chair, waiting for prey.
- See a mouse. Pause and get ready to pounce. Now the mouse is in a good position. Spring and pounce to grab it.
- Oops, the mouse escaped into a mouse hole. Show your feelings.
- Slink over to the mouse hole and poke your paw in to grab the mouse. Reach in as far as you can. You can't get it. Show your feelings.

- Meow in frustration and pad back behind the chair, getting ready for another mouse to come along.

Becoming the Objects

Become these objects by yourself:
- A tree whistling in the wind
- A big, heavy cow mooing
- A tall city building that frightens a country mouse

Become these objects in pairs:
- The elevator going up, coming down, and freezing at the lobby
- A small, round table in the country mouse's house
- A long table in the city mouse's apartment
- City mouse's car
- The mouse hole

What other objects could you be? Show how you could become those objects.

Re-enacting Moments from the Story

Country Mouse's Moments
- Wait on the porch for the city mouse to arrive.
- Serve the city mouse the country meal and wait to see his reaction. What do you say as you serve him?
- Show with your face and body your feelings when the city mouse doesn't like your food.
- Show your feeling as the city mouse drives you over the bumpy roads.

- Look up at the tall "monster" buildings in the city.
- Show your feeling as the elevator zooms up.
- Look at all of the delicious foods.
- Nibble cheeses, gnaw biscuits, and lap up cream.
- Feel the cat's paw on your back and see the hungry cat looking at you.
- In place, scurry into the mouse hole.
- Tell the city mouse, "City life is too fast for me."
- Sit in your rocker — home at last, rocking in the gentle country breeze.

City Mouse's Moments
- Hop onto the elevator and zoom down.
- Jump into your car, slam the door, turn on the key, and rev up the engine, ready for action.
- Bump up and down in the car on the dusty country roads.
- Pant for a soda pop.
- Look around and see that there are no shops, only trees in the country.
- React to the food that the country mouse serves.
- Invite the country mouse to to go to the city for "real food."
- Excitedly point out the big buildings in the city. What could you say about them?
- Point out and describe the different foods to choose from on the table.
- Show surprise that your cousin wants to go home.

Costume Suggestions

Country mouse: A farmer's straw hat and/or red and white neckerchief.
City mouse: A fancy cap or hat and/or bright wild tie.
Cat: White gloves or mittens and/or headband with cat ears.

Critical-Thinking Questions

1. Why do you think the country mouse invited his city cousin to visit?
2. Why didn't the city mouse like the country?
3. What did the country mouse do to try to make the city mouse enjoy the country?
4. What else might the country mouse have done to try to get the city mouse to enjoy the country?
5. What is your opinion about the way the city mouse behaved when he came to the country? Should he have been more polite? Explain.
6. Why did the country mouse feel hurt when the city mouse didn't like her food?
7. What were two things the country mouse disliked about the city? What do you think were her reasons for disliking those things?
8. What was the most upsetting thing that happened to the country mouse? Explain.
9. If the country mouse lived in the city for a year, or if the city mouse lived in the country that long, do you think either might like the other place? Explain what might happen to change their minds.
10. When you grow up, would you prefer to live in the city or country? Explain.
11. What can you do or can you have in the country that you probably can't do or have in the city?
12. What can you do or have in the city that you can't do or have in the country?
13. Why do people who live in the city often like to go to the country for vacation, and people in the country like to vacation in the city?
14. Which mouse would you prefer to have as a friend? Explain.
15. This is one of Aesop's most popular fables. Why do you think both children and adults enjoy it?

Research

- Find a story in which the characters like living in the country. Read it to the class or to another person. Discuss what the characters enjoy about living in the country.
- Find a story in which the characters like living in the city. Read it to the class or to another person. Discuss what the characters enjoy about living in the city.

Creating Art

City or Country? My Preference
Materials:
Cardboard, oaktag, or heavy white paper for backing

Black and colored marking pens
White glue

Magazines, catalogs, postcards, garden-seed packets, fabric, shells, greeting cards, wallpaper

Goal: To make a collage that shows which place each student prefers — the city or the country.

Method: Ask students to decide where they would like to live as an adult — either the city or country. Ask students to bring in magazines, catalogs, post-cards, and other pictures that show their preference.

Have students find other materials such as fabric, theatre tickets, or pretty pebbles to indicate their choices. For example, fabric with small flowers might seem more like the country. Shiny material or sequins might be appropriate for the city.

Tell students that to design their pictures, they should first place a few objects on their papers, then rearrange them until the pattern suits them, and glue the objects on.

Ask students what else they could add. Some students might want to draw objects or figures that represent the city or the country in empty spaces. They could also accent some parts of their collages with marking pen.

On a separate paper, have students write three or more reasons why they prefer either the city or the country. They can tape or glue their reasons to the collage. Ask students to share their collages and tell their reasons for their preferences.

Drama Follow-Up in Pairs
(grades three to six)

Goal: To re-enact the story as a play with the characters only — no narrator, making up dialogue that tells the story.

Have students enact the following scene: The city mouse visits the country mouse's house and does not enjoy it. Then the country mouse visits the city and feels the same way. Have students include the following beginning, middle and ending in their story:

Beginning: The country mouse phones the city mouse and invites him to visit. The city mouse gets directions and is given a time to arrive. The city mouse drives to the country.

Middle: The country mouse points out the trees and serves her cousin a meal. The city mouse turns up his nose at the food and invites the country mouse to the city. The country mouse hides her hurt feelings. Her fur almost jumps off during the drive to the city.

End: The city mouse points out the big buildings. He takes the country mouse into the elevator and up to his apartment to a table with fancy foods. They eat, but are scared by the cat and run into a mouse hole. The country mouse goes home to her rocker, and the city mouse gets ready for a night on the town.

Can you pose like the city mouse? What is he saying?
Can you pose like the country mouse? What could she be saying?

Dramatizing Aesop's Fables

Can you show with your body and face
how each mouse feels here?
Who is the most frightened? Why?

CHAPTER SIX

More Fables to Adapt and Act

The first fable in this chapter, "The Fox and the Grapes," provides a model for adapting literature for dramatization, using the narrative-mime approach.

Questions that follow the fable will help students analyze how the version for dramatization differs from the straight narrative story, and will help them adapt a fable themselves. Twenty-seven of Aesop's fables (chosen because of their dramatic potential) are also provided for teachers or students to adapt and act on their own.

Choosing and Adapting Literature for Narrative Mime

Narrative mime requires a story with characters who are continuously involved in *action*. It helps if these characters are exaggerated, with one or two distinctive traits, such as a crafty, trotting fox or a proud, powerful lion. Humorous material is good for narrative mime because the action and characters are usually broad, and acting out inanimate objects with lively sound effects becomes part of the humor.

Many nonsense story poems, such as "The Adventures of Isabel," by Ogden Nash, and "There Was an Old Lady," by Dennis Lee, have strong characters and lots of action. Almost all Mother Goose rhymes and many limericks can be acted as written.

Fables and simple folk tales in short picture books are ideal choices for the narrative-mime method because they have action in almost every sentence, and clear, broad characters. These books also have vivid pictures that inspire students to become the characters. Many of the picture books by Paul Galdone are well written and illustrated for narrative-mime dramatization.

Most literature benefits from some editing, however, to increase the drama. Unnecessary description should be cut out, and actions and strong feelings should be added.

When adapting literature for narrative mime, think:

How can each sentence or line be dramatized?
How can more action be added to the story?
How can more strong feelings be included for the characters to show?
What objects in the story might have actions to do? Could extra objects and actions be added?

What kind of sound effects would help tell the story? Can an inanimate object be given a sound to make or something to say?

Example of a Fable Adapted for Narrative Mime

The following fable, "The Fox and the Grapes," is written below as a straight narrative story, then rewritten with more actions, feelings, and descriptions of sounds to make it more dramatic. A cast list, sound effects, and costume suggestions are added to create a play.

The Fox and the Grapes
(original version)

As a fox was walking along, he saw a bunch of grapes above him. He wanted the grapes, and hopped up once, twice, three times to get them, but he couldn't quite reach them. He looked again at the grapes and walked away, saying, "They were probably sour anyway."

The Fox and The Grapes
(adapted for narrative mime)

Cast of Characters:
Narrator
Fox
Grapes

Sound-Effects Suggestions: Use a mallet and wood block or tap a desk with a pencil to create the sound of a fox trotting, drum beats for the fox hitting the grapes with a stick, and a triangle for grapes dangling beyond his reach.

A hungry fox was trotting along. He trotted here. He trotted there. He trotted in a circle looking for something to eat. Then he looked up and saw big, purple grapes dangling above him. His tongue hung out, and he drooled. He was excited, and he hopped up and down.

"Yum, yum, yum," he said, rubbing his belly. The fox reached one furry paw up, but he couldn't reach the grapes.

The fox saw a box. He brought the box over to the grapes and stepped onto it. But again the grapes seemed to jump just out of his grasp.

Finally he found a big stick. He climbed on the box and began to hit at the grapes. The grapes swung this way and that, but they wouldn't fall. The fox jumped off the box, raised his fist to the grapes and said, "You were proably sour anyway." The grapes dangled and swung in the breeze. The fox glared at the grapes once more. Then he grumbled and trotted away.

Costume Suggestions:
Fox: red cap
Grapes: purple gloves

Discussing the Narrative-Mime Version of the Fable

1. What action words or verbs were used in the adapted version to give the fox and the grapes more things to do? Underline these action words.
2. What words were added to reveal the fox's feelings and reactions? What were some of the feelings and reactions the fox showed?
3. What actions were added for the grapes?
4. What other objects might have been put in the fable for actors to act?
5. What sound effects were added?
6. What other sound effects could be put in?
7. What other simple costume pieces could be used for the fox or grapes besides a red cap and purple gloves?

Fables to Act and Adapt

The following 27 fables were written to adapt and act. A small group of students might adapt a fable and then act it out.

To Adapt a Fable in Groups

1. Read the fable first.
2. Read each sentence and stop. Does it have action? If not, can you add action?
3. What are the inanimate objects? How could they be dramatized? What can you give them to do or say?
4. Can you add other objects that aren't mentioned in the story? Can you think of something for them to do or say?
5. Can you add sound effects? For example, at what points in the story could the animals make noises showing how they feel?
6. If your fable is short, can you think of a way to make it longer so that the characters can act or talk more?

To Dramatize Your Adapted Fable in Groups

1. Choose a narrator, others to play the characters and objects, and other people to make sound effects.
2. Dramatize the fable.
3. Discuss what you might add or do differently to make your performance more dramatic and theatrical.
4. Rehearse again, trying each other's suggestions.

To Perform Your Adaptation for the Class

1. Read the original version of the fable to the class.
2. Dramatize your adapted fable.
3. Let the class discuss how your adaptation was different from the original.
4. Have the class discuss their positive reactions to your performance. Then they should suggest what might be added or done differently to improve the performance.

5. Rehearse your fable again in groups, trying some of the class's suggestions and adding your own new ideas.

6. Finally, bring in or make simple costume pieces.

7. Use instruments to enhance and accompany the action.

8. Perform your fable for the class again, or visit other classes and put on an Aesop drama festival.

The Kid and the Wolf

A pesky kid (goat) was standing on top of a roof when a wolf came by. The kid yelled at the wolf, "Nyah, nyah, you can't get me. You are a dumb old wolf, anyhow."

The wolf glanced up at the kid and said, "It's not you who are so brave, it's the place you're standing on. If you were on the ground next to me, you'd sing another tune."

The Gardener and His Dog

A gardener was taking water out of his well when his little dog jumped up and fell into the well. The gardener quickly jumped into the well to rescue his dog.

However, just as he brought the dog to the top, the ungrateful beast bit his arm.

"That's no way to treat the hands that saved you," said the gardener. And he dropped the dog back down into the well.

Androcles and the Lion

Androcles was a slave who was cruelly treated by his master. One day he escaped into the woods and came upon a lion. He started to leave, but saw that the lion had a thorn in his paw. Androcles was afraid, but he pulled the thorn out of the lion's paw. The lion was so grateful, he licked Androcles's hand and then led him to a cave for shelter.

The next day, however, both the lion and Androcles were captured by the king's guards and taken to the city to be in the circus. The lion was starved for seven days.

At the end of the seven days the captors brought the hungry lion into the arena. Then they brought in Androcles. Everyone expected the lion to eat the slave. However, the lion bounded over to Androcles, licked his hand, and sat by his side. The watching emperor was so charmed by this reaction that he set both Androcles and the lion free.

The Wolf and the House Dog

A hungry wolf met a well-fed dog walking along the road. She asked the dog how he came to be so well fed. The dog said he had a master who gave him all the food he wanted. All he had to do was guard the master's house.

The wolf thought this sounded like a good arrangement. But as they walked along, she noticed a mark around the dog's neck. She asked the dog what caused the mark. The dog said it was from a collar the master kept on him when he tied him up.

With that, the wolf trotted quickly away, saying, "I'd rather be thin and free than well fed and anyone's slave."

The Mountain in Labor

One day the people in a village heard a rumbling coming from a mountain. Great rocks came crashing down.

They waited and worried, and waited and worried about what would happen. Suddenly a huge crack appeared in the mountain. The people all ran and hid. Finally the fierce noises stopped. Everything was silent. And out of the crack popped a mouse!

The Wolf and the Wise Goat

A wolf saw a goat eating grass near the edge of a cliff. He called in a sweet voice, "Oh, I'm afraid you'll fall from that steep cliff and kill yourself."

The goat went on eating.

Then the wolf said, "It's so windy up there and so peaceful down here."

The goat kept chewing grass.

Finally the wolf said, "I know the grass down here is much sweeter than that up there."

Then the goat said, "I wonder if it is my dinner you're concerned about or your own."

The Fox and the Crow

Once a crow was sitting in a tree, holding a piece of cheese. A fox looked up at the tasty cheese and said, "How beautiful your feathers are, Mr. Crow." With that, the crow ruffled his feathers. Then the fox added, "How glossy your wings are." The crow flapped his wings. Finally, the fox said, "I wonder if your voice is as beautiful as you are. Oh, I wish I could hear it." With that, the vain crow opened his mouth to caw, dropped the cheese, and the fox gobbled it up.

The Ants and the Grasshopper

One summer day, some ants were busily gathering bits of grain and taking them to their home. A grasshopper watched them, and laughed and danced. "Why do you work so hard?" he said.

In a few months, the winds blew, and snow fell, and everyone went inside. One day, the ants heard a knock on the door. It was the grasshopper. "Please give me some food," he said, "I'm starving."

"Why should we?" cried the ants. "You preferred to laugh and dance all summer. You can laugh and dance all winter, too."

The Goose That Laid the Golden Eggs

One day a farmer went to the nest of his goose and found that she had laid a golden egg. He was very excited. Every day from that day on when he went to the barn, there would be another golden egg.

However, the farmer began wishing the goose would lay more than one egg at a time. Finally, he could stand it no more. He picked up an ax and killed the goose in hopes of getting all the eggs at once. Alas, his goose was dead, and there was nothing at all inside.

Hercules and the Wagoner

A farmer was driving a wagon along a muddy road when one wheel got stuck fast in the mud, and the horses could not pull it out.

The farmer got off the wagon and began crying and praying, and begging the god Hercules to come and help him.

Then Hercules appeared and said, "Don't pray to me, lazybones. Put your shoulder to the wheel and pull the wagon out of the mud yourself. The gods help those who help themselves."

The Bundle of Sticks

There was a man who had three children who always quarreled. Their quarrelling was bothering him no end. So he called them together and asked each of them to break a bundle of three sturdy sticks.

Each one tried to break the bundle and failed. The man then gave each child one of the three sticks. Each broke the one stick easily.

The father then asked: "Do you see my lesson? None of you could break the sticks alone, but when you worked together you could do it easily. You are much stronger and more powerful working together than if you are divided and work alone."

The Wolf and the Dancing Kid

One day a bold little kid (goat) did not follow her mother and brothers home. She was thus alone in the woods when a wolf happened along. The wolf grabbed the kid and said he would eat her.

The kid asked if she might be allowed to dance before she died. The wolf liked music before dining, and he began howling and singing while the kid danced. The goatherd's dogs heard the wolf's song and ran to see what was going on. Finding the wolf singing away, and the kid dancing, the dogs bounded at the wolf. He yelped and disappeared into the forest.

"It serves me right; I'm a butcher, not a musician," said the wolf. "I should have stuck to what I know best."

The Donkey and the Load of Salt

A merchant was driving his donkey home with two big bags of salt on her back when they crossed a river, and the donkey slipped and fell in. Immediately, the salt dissolved in the water. When the donkey got up, she had hardly any load at all to carry. This pleased the donkey.

The next day, the merchant again put salt on the donkey's back. This time when the frisky donkey got to the river, she purposefully fell into the water to get rid of the salt.

The angry merchant took the donkey back to town and loaded her back with big sponges. The next time the donkey fell into the river, she had ten times more to bear, because the sponges were now heavy with water.

The Dog in the Manger

A dog lying in a manger filled with hay was awakened by a hungry cow. The cow mooed, and politely asked the dog to move over so that she could eat some hay.

The dog snarled and growled and would not move. The cow asked the dog why he was so selfish, since he didn't even eat hay.

The farmer saw what was going on. He grabbed a stick and drove the dog out of the manger for his selfishness. "You are a mean cur to prevent someone from having something you don't even want," the farmer said.

The Travelers and the Shade Tree

Two travelers were walking along on a hot day. They sat down under a big tree to cool off.

One looked up at the tree and exclaimed, "What a useless tree you are. You don't give fruits or nuts for people to eat."

With that the tree bowed down its branches and replied, "I am being very useful now, cooling you from the rays of the hot sun."

The Doctor Wolf

A wolf once cornered a donkey and said he was going to eat her. The donkey said she'd be happy to be eaten, but she asked the wolf to first remove the thorn in her hoof so it wouldn't scratch the wolf's throat.

The wolf said it was most thoughtful of the donkey to be concerned about his throat. He then bent over to pull out the thorn, but the donkey gave him a swift kick and trotted away. "It serves me right," said the wolf. "I'm a wolf, not a doctor. I should stick to what I know."

The Fox and the Hen

A fox crept into a hen house. Seeing a fine-looking hen on a roost, he called, "You don't look too well today, Mrs. Red. Why don't you fly down and let me take your pulse?"

The hen fluffed her feathers, looked down, and said, "You're right, Mr. Fox. I am not feeling very well now. And I'll feel a lot better when you trot out the door."

The Fox and the Cicada

A cicada was singing a happy song one evening when a fox passed under the tree on which she was sitting.

"You are a beautiful singer," said the fox. "Please come down here so I can admire the way you look, too."

The wise cicada tossed down a leaf, and immediately the fox pounced on it. "You gave yourself away," she said. "I have never trusted you since the day I saw broken cicada wings under my tree."

The Mother Goat and Her Kids

A mother goat went out one day, leaving her kids at home. "Keep the house shut up tight," the mother said. "There's a nasty wolf in the neighborhood."

Dramatizing Aesop's Fables

The wolf had been lurking around and heard what the mother said. When she left, he sneaked up to the house and knocked. Disguising his voice to sound mother-like, he said, "Let me in, children. I'm your mother. The wolf is after me."

The wise kids stood on their hind feet and peered out the window. Sure enough, it was the wolf peeking through the key hole.

"Get out of here," called the kids. "You sound like our mother, but you look like a wolf."

The Boy Who Cried Wolf

There was once a shepherd boy who liked to play tricks. He got bored going to the mountain with his sheep every day, so he decided to have a bit of fun and pretend that a wolf was after the sheep. "Wolf, wolf," he called, "A wolf is after my sheep!"

The villagers all came running, but then the boy cried, "Ha, ha, ha! There was no wolf. I was only kidding."

The following two days the boy did the same thing, and each time the villagers ran to help him.

Finally one day a real wolf came along and did begin to attack the sheep. "Wolf, wolf," called the shepherd boy. But no one came to help him. Soon the wolf had run off with all the sheep.

The Lazy Donkey

A man bought a donkey at the market with the bargain that he could bring her back in a day, if she did not meet his satisfaction. The man already owned two other donkeys — one, a hard-working, loyal donkey, and another, a lazy one who would do no work.

The man led the new donkey to the barn. The new donkey sniffed both of her new companions, and then she walked over to the lazy one and began eating with her.

With that, the man took the donkey back to the market. The merchant asked how he could have tested the donkey's work in such a short time.
"I don't need to test her work," the man replied. "I could tell what she's like by the company she keeps."

The Candle

A red candle was boasting one night that it shone brighter than the sun, the moon, and the stars combined. With that, a blast of wind came through the door and blew the candle out.

The woman who lit it again said, "I've never seen the sun, the moon, or the stars blown out by a puff of wind."

The Fir Tree and the Bramble

A fir tree bragged to a bramble how much better she was than he was. "You are such a low plant," she said. "Look at me, I'm so tall, strong, and beautiful."

"Yes, you are," said the bramble. "But when woodcutters come, I'd much prefer to be a simple bramble still standing than a fir tree knocked to the ground by a heavy ax."

The Horse and the Burdened Donkey

There was man who had a beautiful horse and a hard-working donkey. Each day, the man rode the horse, while the donkey carried the man's heavy bundles weighing three times the man's weight.

One hot day the donkey was not feeling well, and she asked the horse to help her share the burden. The haughty horse said she had her own job, and that was carrying the master, and that was all that she would do.

The donkey trudged on in silence, but suddenly her thin legs gave way under the burden and she collapsed. Now the horse had to carry the master and all of the burden, and in addition she was deprived of a friendly companion.

The Bear and the Bees

A bear was walking through the woods when a bee stung him. The bear was so angry that he decided to seek revenge on the whole bee family. He went to the beehive and whacked it with his paw. At that, all the bees in the family attacked him, and he had to run and dive in the river. When he came out, he was still covered with stings. "I should have overlooked what the one bee did and not have caused the whole pack of them to come after me," he said.

The Dissatisfied Buck

A deer used to go to the brook every day and admire the reflection of his antlers in the water. He believed his antlers to be his most beautiful feature. He was ashamed, however, when he looked at his legs, finding them too skinny.

One day while the deer was admiring his antlers, he heard a pack of hounds running after him. He rushed into the forest and his antlers got caught in the branches of a tree. He was trapped. "I should have admired my legs that could have saved me, rather than these antlers that have done me in," he thought.

The Donkey and the Thistles

A donkey was munching some thistles when a crow came by and cawed, "Ha, ha, ha, what a miserable diet you have. Can't you find any better food than tough thistles?"

But the donkey kept munching and said, "I'll tell you, to me these thistles are the most delicious food in the world."

CHAPTER SEVEN

Developing Reading Through Dramatization

This chapter describes three ways to use Aesop's fables to develop reading skills.

Pair/Shared Reading Approach

The pair/shared reading approach uses the fables in this book as they are written. One student is the reader-narrator and the other is the actor. This approach is similar to the Everybody Plays All the Parts method, except that this time one student (rather than the whole class) acts all the parts.

The reader's job is to read with excitement and to pause to give the actor a chance to act every part read. This method could be used with a reader as the narrator and a nonreader as the actor. If both students can read well, they might take turns acting and reading.

Script-Making Methods

Two script-making methods, narrated play script and story theatre, can be used to introduce drama to self-conscious older students, who feel more secure at first reading from a script. These methods also demonstrate how to create simple scripts from stories and how to practice both reading and drama.

A difficulty with acting while holding scripts, however, is that the script may hinder students from fully using their bodies.

Students might first do the Becoming the Character warm-up activities and get ready to act. They might also brainstorm movements with each other or the teacher to think of ways to make movements while still holding scripts. It often takes practice to coordinate both reading and acting.

Narrated Play Script

A narrated script means that every line in the story is given either to a narrator who describes the action or to one of the characters, who simply says his or her own dialogue.

To make a narrated play script:
- Choose a fable to adapt.
- Assign one or more narrators. Write Narrator: or N: next to the narrators' parts.

- Place characters' names or an abbreviation next to their dialogue.
- Eliminate unnecessary attributions such as, "He said," "She said."

Example

Narrator One: "The Crow and the Pitcher" by Aesop
Narrator Two: A beautiful black crow was flying in the hot sun.
Narrator Three: The sun was burning its rays onto his body.
Narrator Four: The crow landed and fanned himself with a wing.
Narrator One: Then he hopped along looking for water.
Crow: Where's the water? Where's the water?

Story Theatre

With story theatre, developed by actor Paul Sills, the story is also used as written, but every sentence is assigned to the character who might say it. Story theatre uses no narrator. Characters describe the action that is happening to them, say their dialogue, and perform their actions at the same time.
To create a story-theatre script:
- Choose a fable to act.
- Assign each sentence, even the title, to a character to say.

Example

Dog: "The Dog and His Reflection." Once a greedy dog was trotting by a butcher's shop. He looked in the window and saw a big steak on the counter. His eyes grew big. His tongue hung out. He wanted that steak.
Dog: I want that steak.
Butcher: The butcher was waiting on a customer.
Customer: The customer pointed to the steak she wanted.
Butcher: The butcher turned to get paper for the steak.
Dog: The dog slunk into the butcher's shop. He seized the steak in his teeth and trotted out the door.
Butcher and Customer: The butcher and the customer ran out yelling.
Butcher and Customer: Stop! Stop!

Students can easily make their own scripts. Simply copy a fable from this book and let small groups decide how to assign each sentence. The groups can then practice their scripts and perform them for the class.

CHAPTER EIGHT

Critical Thinking and New Projects

The following questions, art, and research projects can be used with any fable or group of fables. Students might use the 8 adapted fables and the 27 original fables in this book to do these activities. They might also use some of the numerous editions of Aesop's fables in libraries. The picture books are valuable to compare different art styles and to inspire students' own art. The bibliography lists picture books with individual or several fables and large collections with a hundred or more. It also includes translations of the fables in Spanish and a picture book of Native American fables adapted from Aesop.

Critical-Thinking Questions

1. What is the moral of the fable? (Interpretations will vary. Over the centuries, there have been differing interpretations of the same fable and often more than one moral.)
2. Who in the fable learns something? What does that character learn? (Often both main characters and sometimes even minor ones learn something.)
3. Why do you think most fables are short? How would they be weakened if they were much longer?
4. Would you prefer a fable to state its moral at the end, or would you rather decide for yourself what it means? Explain.
5. What is Aesop trying to teach people?

Reading, Research, and Comparison Activities

1. Find two fables with the same animal as a major character. For example, find two featuring a lion, a fox, or a crow as the main character. Read the two fables aloud to the class. Explain how the main character acts differently or the same in both fables. Is the lion, for example, proud or domineering in both fables? Is he tricky in one fable and not in the other?
2. Find fables with the same or similar moral or theme. Read them to a partner or to the class. For example, find more than one fable that shows:
   • One bad turn deserves another.
   • The smallest becomes the most powerful.
   • Don't be greedy.

- Persistence pays off.
- Don't be taken in by flatterers.
- One good turn deserves another.
- One man's meat is another man's poison.
- Pride goeth before a fall.

3. Get a book of the fables of La Fontaine, a famous French fabulist, or fable-teller. La Fontaine wrote in rhymed couplets. What are rhymed couplets? Read one of his fables aloud. What is your opinion of the rhymed couplets? Do you think they are a good technique to use to tell a fable? Explain.

4. Some of La Fontaine's fables are adapted directly from Aesop. Find a La Fontaine fable that is similar to one by Aesop, such as "The Town Mouse and the Country Mouse," "The Fox and the Grapes," or "The Hen That Laid the Golden Eggs." How are the two fables the same? How are they different? Which do you like better, and why?

Writing

1. Choose a fable with two main characters. List all the words you can think of to describe each of the two characters. Then tell which one you would prefer to have as a friend and why.

2. Study the fables of Aesop and Arnold Lobel, a modern American fabulist. What are the characteristics of a fable? Write a fable. Perhaps the class can write one together. Then write your own fable or write one with a partner. If possible, act it out for the class.

Illustration Research

Research picture books of Aesop's fables. Pick out one illustrator whom you like very much. Tell the class why you like this illustrator and why you think she or he is a good illustrator of Aesop's fables.

Art Activities

Class Mural of Aesop's fables

After dramatizing different fables in groups, let students in each group illustrate a dramatic scene from the fable they have acted. Put the scenes from the different fables on a class mural.

In their groups, let students decide what scene they want to illustrate and who in the group will illustrate which character or part of the setting. For example, using "The Hare and the Tortoise," one student would draw the tortoise; another, the hare; and the rest, other animals or whatever else they need in the scene.

Have students first sketch on the mural in pencil, and then paint it when they are satisfied with their drawing. Or have them draw and color their parts individually, cut them out, and paste them on their section of the mural.

The background could be a general forest scene to give the painting unity.

Someone might be assigned to draw Aesop as that person thinks he might have looked. Let the class decide where to place Aesop on the mural.

A Theatrical Poster

Have students make a theatrical poster advertising a performance of one or more of Aesop's fables. Tell them to determine which fables they want to perform and then draw something from one, some, or all of those fables that will interest the audience in wanting to see the show. Have students think of a slogan to announce the show. Tell them not to forget the time, place, date of performance, and the fee if there is to be one.

A Birthday Card for Aesop

Say to students, "We don't know Aesop's birthday. Pretend it's tomorrow. Make Aesop a birthday card he would enjoy. Or make Aesop a thank-you card for a fable you enjoyed."

Bibliography

Collections with 50 or More Fables

Artzybasheff, Boris (illus). *Aesop's Fables*. Viking Press, 1945. Illustrations are charming wood engravings.

Ash, Russell, and Bernard Highton. *Aesop's Fables, A Classic Illustrated Edition*. Chronicle Books, 1990. Art is provided by famous illustrators of the last 100 years.

Baber, Frank. *The Fables of Aesop, 149 Moral Tales Retold*. Illustrated by Ruth Spriggs. Rand McNally and Company, 1975. Realistic pictures help students become the characters.

Jacobs, Joseph, editor. *The Fables of Aesop*. Illustrated by Richard Heighway. (first published 1894) Schoken Books, Inc., 1966. Includes history of fables and humorous pen and ink drawings by nine famous illustrators. This collection is especially good for grades five and above.

Kredel, Fritz. *Aesop's Fables*. Grosset and Dunlap, 1947. This collection includes 154 fables with subtle evocative drawings in both pen and ink and color.

Tinklelman, Murray. *Aesop's Fables*. Doubleday, 1986. The witty translation by George Tyler Townsend and the informative introduction by Isaac Bashevis Singer add to the enjoyment of the fables.

Winter, Milo. *The Aesop for Children*. Rand McNally, 1984. (first published 1919) Includes over 100 fables with realistic color pictures. Appeals to all ages.

Picture Books with 10 to 20 Fables

Alley, Robert M. *Seven Fables from Aesop*. Dodd, 1986. Includes "The Lion and the Mouse," "The Wind and the Sun," "The Dog and His Reflection," and "The Hare and the Tortoise." Sweet pictures appeal to kindergarten through grade two.)

Chapman, Graynor. *Aesop's Fables*. Atheneum, 1972. Familiar and unfamiliar fables are illustrated with unusual color prints.

Hague, Michael. *Aesop's Fables*. Henry Holt and Company, Inc., 1985. This popular edition includes "The Lion and the Mouse," "The Town Mouse and the Country Mouse," "The Crow and the Pitcher," "The Hare and the Tortoise," "The Fox and the Grapes," and others.

Holder, Heidi. *Aesop's Fables*. Viking, 1981. "The Hare and the Tortoise," "The Country Mouse and the City Mouse," "The Fox and the Grapes," and three lesser-known fables are illustrated with elegant pen-and-ink drawings finished in water color.

Paxton, Tom. *Aesop's Fables Retold in Verse*. Illustrated by Robert Rayevsky. Morrow, 1988. Witty verses are illustrated with animals in Renaissance costumes.

Rice, Eve. *Once in a Wood: Ten Tales from Aesop*. Greenwillow, 1980. Includes "The Fox and the Crow," "The Lion and the Mouse," "The Fox and the Stork," and "The Crow and the Water Jug." Second-or third-grade reading level. The fables are often illustrated in several scenes.

Santore, Charles. *Aesop's Fables*. Crown Books, Jellybean Press, 1988. The art in this large book is highly imaginative.

Svend, Otto S. *Aesop: The Fox and the Stork, Twenty Fables Illustrated*. Pelham Books Ltd., 1985. Characters are illustrated in action with large pictures.

Testa, Fulvio. *Aesop's Fables*. Barron's, 1989. Includes "The Fox and the Stork," "The Lion and the Mouse," "The Tortoise and the Hare," "The Fox and the Grapes," "The Fox and Crow," and others with bright, inviting illustrations.

Watson, Carol. *Aesop's Fables Retold*. Illustrated by Nick Price. Usborne Publishers Ltd., 1982. Ten fables are illustrated in delightful comic strip style, appealing to all age levels.

Picture Books with Single Fables

Castle, Caroline, *The Hare and the Tortoise*. Illustrated by Peter Weevers. Dial Books, 1985. An athletic Hare and a day-dreaming writer Tortoise are illustrated in graceful water colors.

Cauley, Lorinda Bryan. *The Town Mouse and the Country Mouse*. G. P. Putnam's Sons, 1984. Lyrical pictures depict the two characters and their respective environments.

Galdone, Paul. *The Hare and the Tortoise*. McGraw-Hill, 1962. Dynamic, humorous illustrations by this illustrator always inspire characterization.

_____. *The Town Mouse and the Country Mouse*. McGraw-Hill, 1971.

_____. *Three Aesop Fox Tales*. The Seabury Press, 1971. Includes "The Fox and the Grapes," "The Fox and the Stork," and "The Fox and the Crow."

Stevens, Janet. *The Hare and the Tortoise*. Holiday House, 1984. Witty, contemporary drawings of the animals illustrate a lively telling of the fable.

_____. *The Town Mouse and the Country Mouse*. Holiday House, 1987. A party-girl city mouse and a down-home-boy country mouse appeal to all ages.

Wildsmith, Brian. *The Lion and the Rat*. Franklin Watts, 1963. Excellent pictures help with dramatization.

_____. *The North Wind and the Sun*. Franklin Watts, 1964. Vivid pictures illustrate the contest.

Young, Ed. *The Lion and the Mouse*. Doubleday, 1980. The tale is told from the mouse's point of view.

Fable Books of Other Cultures

Bierhorst, John, adaptor. *Doctor Coyote, A Native American Aesop's Fables*. Macmillan, 1987. Aesop's fables are retold by Aztec Indians, using Coyote as the main character. Amusing colorful drawings provide an excellent way to show Aesop's influence on a different culture.

La Fontaine, Jean de. *Fifty Fables of La Fontaine*, translated by Norman R. Shapiro. University of Illinois Press, 1988. The famous French fabulist's rhymed couplets are given in both the original French and the English translation.

Lobel, Arnold. *Fables*. Harper & Row, 1980. Delightful modern American fables are humorously illustrated in this Caldecott winner.

Aesop's Fables in Spanish

Benilliure, Graciela Ines. *Fabulas de Esopo*, Editorial Concepto, S. A. A. U. Cuauhtemac, Mexico, 1979.

Kincaid, Lucy, adaptor. *Fabulas de Siempre, Seleccion de Fabulas de Esopo*. Illustrated by Eric Kincaid. Editorial Everest, S. A. Brimax Rights Ltd., 1981.

El Marvilloso Mundo de las Fabulas. Editorial, Alfred Otells, S. L., 1986.

Books To Inspire Animal Characterization

ZOO BOOKS publishes 58 inexpensive magazines, each specializing in one animal or animal family. The large photographs and realistic drawings with fascinating information about the animals help students "become" animals. For a list of available topics and to order magazines, write to Wildlife Education, 590 Kettner Blvd., San Diego, CA 92101.

Creative Drama Books for Use in the Classroom

Cook, Wayne. *Center Stage: A Curriculum for the Performing Arts*. Dale Seymour Publications, 1993. One volume is for kindergarten through grade three and another is for grades four through six. Thirty sequential lessons per grade level lead students and teacher from exploratory activities to fully developed creative dramatics.

Heinig, Ruth Beall. *Creative Drama For the Classroom Teacher*, third edition. Prentice Hall, 1988. Several ways to dramatize literature are described. The author also shows how to use creative drama in the classroom to enrich the curriculum. (kindergarten to grade six)

Nobleman, Roberta. *Mime and Masks*. New Plays Incorporated, 1979. Box 5074, Charlottesville, VA 22905. Inventive mime activities and directions for making simple masks are included. (all grades)

Novelly, Maria C. *Theatre Games For Young Performers*. Meriwether Publishing Ltd., 1985. P.O. Box 7710, Colorado Springs, CO 80933. Simple drama activities on pantomime and voice include how to read effectively aloud, improvisation, and scene building. (geared to upper grades)

Sher, Anna, and Charles Verralle. *100+ Ideas for Drama*. Heineman Educational Books, 1975. Succinctly stated activities often require virtually no teacher preparation time. Activities for all grades are included.

Books to Help Students Draw Animals

Benjamin, Carol Lea. *Cartooning for Kids*. Thomas Y. Crowell, 1982. How to draw cartoon animals is described in this appealing book with delightful illustrations. Enjoyable for all grades. Even kindergartners might be able to make the simple animal faces.

Emberley, Ed. *Ed Emberley's Drawing Book of Animals*. Little, Brown & Co., 1970. This delightful, useful book shows how to use shapes, letters, numbers, and other markings to draw many animals.

Emberley, Rebecca. *Drawing with Numbers and Letters*. Little, Brown & Co., 1981. The author shows how to put numbers and letters together to draw fanciful animals. (grades 1 to 6)

Ames, Lee J. *Draw 50 Animals*. Doubleday, 1974. This book will be helpful for fourth to sixth graders who want to make realistic animals.